Cathal J Finnegan is a singer, songwriter, and is currently in the process of building a music streaming platform for independent artists. He resides in Ireland with his wife and two children, Aaron and Maggy.

He completed his law degree in 2019 and subsequently completed all eight FE1 Irish Law Society exams, which are a prerequisite for obtaining a training contract with an Irish law firm. He is currently studying to sit the California Bar Exam.

In summing up, he is passionate about tackling injustice in the music arena and also in the area of employment law. You can check out his most recent book *Tech Thief* which is available on Amazon which shines a light on the author's experience of being defrauded by his music distributor CD Baby, in the area of music royalties.

I wish to dedicate this book to David Duke, my former colleague at The Abbey Hotel, Roscommon.

David was killed in a tragic accident on Wednesday, 27th January, 2021.

David's gentle spirit taught me what true power is. During his time at the Abbey hotel, he was oil on troubled waters, a light in the dark and a listening ear to those who carried heavy burdens.

David had an aura and a presence that brought comfort to many a troubled soul at the Abbey hotel.

When it came to standing up the bullyboys at the Abbey hotel, David was more than a match for them and made it clear to them that he was not going to be intimidated. And finally, David was the best co-worker I ever worked with.

"Don't stay in a toxic work culture. Don't settle for less than you deserve. The right place will value you in the right way."
(Gary Travis @Gary Travis on Linkedin)

Cathal J Finnegan

Rockstar Porter

Faith Under Pressure

Copyright © Cathal J Finnegan 2022

The right of Cathal J Finnegan to be identified as author of this work has been asserted by the author in accordance with the copyright Act of 2000 in this jurisdiction.

All rights reserved. No part of this publication may be reproduced, stored in a retrieval system, or transmitted in any form or by any means, electronic, mechanical, photocopying, recording, or otherwise, without the prior permission of the publishers.

Any person who commits any unauthorised act in relation to this publication may be liable to criminal prosecution and civil claims for damages.

I would like to thank my wife Marketa who offered valuable insights on pricing the book and is responsible for the foxy picture on the front of the book.

I would like to extend a big thank you to Jack Danson, Layla Wandsworth and Brent Hayworth and Carl Carpenter, my former colleagues at the Abbey Hotel, Roscommon, for clarifying certain matters and ensuring that key aspects of the book were factually correct.

To all my former colleagues at the Abbey Hotel who are out of work due to the coronavirus, my thoughts are with you. I pray that during this crisis you will use this book as a light in the dark to guide you through this dark spell that has engulfed the world. I pray that God will use it to reshape your thinking and help you come out of this trial stronger.

.

Table of Contents

Foreword	15
Introduction	17
Part 1: I'm a Porter, Get Me Out of Here	22
Chapter 1: Meet the Grealy Family	23
Chapter 2: The Staff	32
Chapter 3: A Door of Hope	48
Chapter 4: Wolves in Sheep's Clothing	52
Chapter 5: A Dirty Little Secret	57
Chapter 6: A Hidden Epidemic	62
Part 2: Verdict please	60
Chapter 7: A Legal Perspective	73
Chapter 8: Tick-Box Exercises	80
Chapter 9: Harassment (including sexual harassment)	85
Chapter 10: Fair Procedures	95
Chapter 11: Dodgy Director's and Fraud	106
Chapter 12: Health and Safety	113
Chapter 13: Invasion of Privacy	119
Part 3: Let's Go Deep	133
Chapter 14: Brothers at War	135

Chapter 15: Rooting Out Toxicity	141
Part 4: Time for Change	145
Chapter 16: Make My Day Punk	147
Chapter 17: The Day of Battle	152
Chapter 18: Appeal to the Labour Court	155
Chapter 19: Setback	163
Part 5: Breaking the Cycle	171
Chapter 20: Beating the Fear Factor	173
Chapter 21: A Paradigm Shift	176
Chapter 22: The Legal Profession	181

Disclaimer

This book represents the views and opinions of the author. For professional legal advice please speak to a qualified lawyer. Every effort has been made to ensure that the content of this book is factual and up to date and that it is not defamatory in any way. I have made every effort to ensure it respects and abides by the legislation laid down in the Defamation Act of 2009 in Ireland.

Foreword

For the most part, forewords are usually written by somebody famous in order to give the reader confidence that the author actually knows what they are talking about and ultimately to convince you to buy the book. However, after much meditation and prayer I have decided to put this book out without anybody famous writing the foreword. Why? This book is a prophetic word to employers. It is a strong and uncompromising word that will tackle thorny issues and uncomfortable truths, particularly bullying in this jurisdiction.

"Son of man, prophesy against the shepherds, the leaders of Israel. Give them this message from the Sovereign Lord: What sorrow awaits you shepherds who feed yourselves instead of your flocks." (Ezekiel 34 v 2)

Introduction

Where did the idea come from to write this book? Well just a quick rewind before I go into the book. On August 23rd, 2018 I walked out of my employment and nine weeks later I filed a constructive dismissal lawsuit against my employer. A few months later, I was resting on my bed when this bright idea came to write a book about my six years at the Abbey Hotel, Roscommon, Ireland. This was going to be my insurance policy should the Irish legal system not find in my favour.

I came up with the title *Rockstar Porter, Faith Under Pressure*. It sounded dramatic! One of the key issues I will be addressing in these memoirs is how harshly the staff were treated by the Grealy family. In the 2013 report *(Physical & psychological violence at the workplace: Publications office of the European Union, Luxembourg)* Ireland (my native country), was named the 7th worst country in Europe for workplace bullying. I share this statistic to put you on notice that Ireland, and indeed many nations, have a problem with workplace bullying.

Other topics I will touch upon are violations of company law and GDPR for CCTV.

We are currently riding a potential global disaster in the form of the coronavirus. It has affected many industries, particularly the hotel and catering industry. I pray that the coronavirus will have caused employers to assess the way they treat their employees and that their hearts are softer.

The GOAL or OBJECTIVE of this book is five-fold

1) To highlight the issue of bullying in the workplace.
2) To envision employers as to the treasures that they have in their employees and to see employees as assets and not a cost to the business.
3) To empower employees in the workplace.
4) To root out toxic leaders and individuals from your organisation.
5) For the legal profession, I hope this book will better enable you to better serve your clients whether they are an employee or employer.

The primary thrust of this book is point number 1, *"highlighting bullying in the workplace"*. It is causing untold stress in the workplace. Most people spend eight hours a day at work. It is a large chunk of one's day. It is my hope that by sharing my memoirs, we can tackle this hidden shame in Ireland. It is one of Ireland's dirty little secrets. It is time to shine the light of truth on this cowardly spirit of bullying in our nation and kick it out.

Each chapter will conclude with a lesson learned and a spiritual insight to strengthen you along the road of life. There will also be a short exercise at the end of each chapter to complete. This is optional, but I recommend you do it. Heck you paid for the book; might as well get your money's worth.

In the next chapter, I will introduce you to my former employer. I recommend strong coffee from here on in. Some of you may need or prefer something stronger! You can party like 1999 to celebrate the release of this book.

"Behold I am doing a new thing; now it springs forth, do you not perceive it? I will make a way in the wilderness and rivers in the desert." (Isaiah 43 v 19)

Part 1
I'm a Porter, Get Me Out of Here

Chapter 1
Meet the Grealy Family

"A family is a social system and if that system is dysfunctional, the ramifications for the child are grave and by the time children have grown up, dysfunction has been deeply ingrained in mind, body and brain." [1]

If vampires actually existed I am convinced my employer could trace their blood line back to these blood sucking creatures. Well the first four months at the Abbey were tough to say the least. While it was not the first hotel I had worked in, the management style was one which could only be described as totalitarian.

---

[1] Christopher Dines *"Drug, addiction recovery, the mindful way"* (2019)

It was a toxic atmosphere with all the classic elements of aggression, abuse, intimidation, fear and control which enabled the Grealy family to violate employment and company law with impunity. It became clear that I was dealing with a dysfunctional family in the Grealys. Let me introduce you to some of the crazy characters running the Abbey Hotel.

First up is Tom Grealy Senior who is the second generation of Grealys. His father founded the business in the 1960s. Legend has it that he won it in a poker game. How true this is, I don't know. This chap features later in the chapter on CCTV.

And now for a funny story to set the tone! This book is the hybrid version of Fawlty Towers [2] and Downton Abbey. [3]Back in 2017, a lady, at a wedding, came up to Senior Day Porter, Jack Danson, and asked, *"Do you know that man over there, he looks lost; is he homeless?"* Senior Day Porter, Jack Danson, replied, *"that is the owner."* True story! Just setting the tone folks!

Tom Senior's wife, Anya, is originally from Cork and started out as an air-hostess and has a posh accent, not the kind

---
[2] https://en.wikipedia.org/wiki/Downton_Abbey
[3] https://en.wikipedia.org/wiki/Fawlty_Towers

of accent you would associate with a person from Cork. She has a 'reputation' as a business woman and presents herself as the lady of the manor. However, this myth will be blown out of the water later on in the book. I was advised when I started at the Abbey Hotel to never fall out with her. In the years to follow, I was to find out the truth of this advice. Writing this book is like testing to see if the unstoppable force (that is Cathal J. Finnegan) will blow away the apparently immoveable 'object' that is the Abbey hotel.

Next is Adrian Grealy, their son and one of four children. It became clear from early on that this guy was a complete madman. This was a chap it seemed that was allowed to roam around like a lion, attacking staff verbally without restraint. He was into motor rallying.

When I arrived at the Abbey in September 2012, no one would have thought we were in the middle of a recession. It was like a scene from the swinging 1920s film, *'The Great Gatsby'*. [4]Adrian had an air of swag and bravado about him and resembled one of those mad characters from '

---

[4] https://www.imdb.com/title/tt1343092/ and
https://www.sparknotes.com/lit/gatsby/

The Wolf of Wall Street', played by Leonardo Di Caprio, who constantly partied. [5]

Then there was Tom Junior, the guy in the pink shirt. He would stroll in at 10 am in the morning with his earphones on. The staff member who would be on duty would dread those 20 minutes in the morning looking at his sour and grumpy face. He would request a coffee and scones, or maybe toast. Then he would watch some golf on the television in the bar. Yes folks, Tom couldn't function without his bit of golf on television in the morning.

So what was the straw that broke the camels' back between me and Tom Grealy Junior? It was the summer of 2017 when I had enough of this sorry excuse for a man. One day, as I went to the kitchen to pick up something to eat, I realised that there was nothing left for the staff, so I headed up to the carvery. It was about 2.45 pm, which is closing time for the carvery on a week-day. There wasn't exactly a whole lot left in the carvery either. I managed to get two vegetable

---
[5] https://www.imdb.com/title/tt0993846/

tartlets and some coleslaw. I proceeded to leave the carvery and walked through the kitchen. I stopped at the end of the kitchen to pick up cutlery. It was at that point I realised Tom Grealy Junior had followed me and observed what was on my plate. I proceeded to the canteen. Grace Kiely, who ran the carvery three days a week, blasted through the door a few minutes later, looking rather disturbed. She asked me if she upset me. I said no, but the dickhead that is Tom Grealy Junior did.

This is a guy who managed to verbally abuse Lily Brackstone in the bar many years ago. But hey, his mother came to the rescue. She (Anya Grealy) apologised on behalf of her son and pleaded with Lily Brackstone to come back to the Abbey.

This Tom Grealy Junior will become central to the reason why I left the Abbey Hotel and was eventually forced to take a constructive dismissal case against the Abbey Hotel.

My contract with the Abbey Hotel pretty much left my employer with a lot of latitude. It's why the relationship between employer and employee is considered to be one of *'an inequality of arms'*.

The employer essentially has the upper hand. However, my long-term goal in the area of employment law is to level the playing field by giving you, the employee, the knowledge and the tools to deal with inequality in the workplace.

Indeed I encourage you to follow my law page @cathalslawpage on Facebook. The page was set up in September 2018 to give employees knowledge to equip them in the workplace. The Grealy family were allowed to get away with so much for so long because nobody wanted the hassle of standing up to them. I find it quite shocking that people in employment these days will allow their employer to piss on them and demean them so much.

It is a sad reflection on the Irish people, considering our forefathers rose up and drove the British out and purchased our independence in blood. It is time to rise up if you are being bullied and take back control of your life! I intend to invoke the spirit of Jim Larkin who spoke up for workers' rights. [6]

POBLACHT NA H EIREANN.
THE PROVISIONAL GOVERNMENT
OF THE
IRISH REPUBLIC
TO THE PEOPLE OF IRELAND.

IRISHMEN AND IRISHWOMEN In the name of God and of the dead generations from which she receives her old tradition of nationhood, Ireland, through us, summons her children to her flag and strikes for her freedom.

Having organised and trained her manhood through her secret revolutionary organisation, the Irish Republican Brotherhood, and through her open military organisations, the Irish Volunteers and the Irish Citizen Army, having patiently perfected her discipline, having resolutely waited for the right moment to reveal itself, she now seizes that moment, and, supported by her exiled children in America and by gallant allies in Europe, but relying in the first on her own strength, she strikes in full confidence of victory.

We declare the right of the people of Ireland to the ownership of Ireland, and to the unfettered control of Irish destinies, to be sovereign and indefeasible. The long usurpation of that right by a foreign people and government has not extinguished the right, nor can it ever be extinguished except by the destruction of the Irish people. In every generation the Irish people have asserted their right to national freedom and sovereignty; six times during the past three hundred years they have asserted it in arms. Standing on that fundamental right and again asserting it in arms in the face of the world, we hereby proclaim the Irish Republic as a Sovereign Independent State, and we pledge our lives and the lives of our comrades-in-arms to the cause of its freedom, of its welfare, and of its exaltation among the nations.

The Irish Republic is entitled to, and hereby claims, the allegiance of every Irishman and Irishwoman. The Republic guarantees religious and civil liberty, equal rights and equal opportunities to all its citizens, and declares its resolve to pursue the happiness and prosperity of the whole nation and of all its parts, cherishing all the children of the nation equally, and oblivious of the differences carefully fostered by an alien government, which have divided a minority from the majority in the past.

Until our arms have brought the opportune moment for the establishment of a permanent National Government, representative of the whole people of Ireland and elected by the suffrages of all her men and women, the Provisional Government, hereby constituted, will administer the civil and military affairs of the Republic in trust for the people.

We place the cause of the Irish Republic under the protection of the Most High God, Whose blessing we invoke upon our arms, and we pray that no one who serves that cause will dishonour it by cowardice, inhumanity, or rapine. In this supreme hour the Irish nation must, by its valour and discipline and by the readiness of its children to sacrifice themselves for the common good, prove itself worthy of the august destiny to which it is called.

Signed on Behalf of the Provisional Government,
THOMAS J. CLARKE.
SEAN Mac DIARMADA.   THOMAS MacDONAGH.
P. H. PEARSE.   EAMONN CEANNT.
JAMES CONNOLLY.   JOSEPH PLUNKETT.

In my first job as an operative in Kepak, Athleague, Roscommon, I dropped my tools and walked out. That was at age 19 in 1991. Even then, I valued myself and NO employer was ever going to walk over me.

---

[6] https://en.wikipedia.org/wiki/James_Larkin

What is even more remarkable is that since then, we have had so much legislation in the area of employment enacted by our parliament to protect the rights of workers. One would think that employees would fight for their rights. Even in the area of Tort law, employees can sue for damages if they are hurt, which includes stress related illnesses induced by stress at work which goes beyond acceptable levels. I will now introduce you to the staff of the Abbey Hotel in the next chapter. Some are absolute legends while others were complete bastards! But not before you absorb another spiritual vitamin!

Scripture: *"And if a house is divided against itself, that house cannot stand."* (Mark 3 v25)

Lesson: The Grealy family consisted of four family members, each with a differing vision to the other for the hotel. Without unity of heart, your family or business will eventually crumble, unless all of you share the same vision.

Exercise – Write down the name of your first employer. That could be your first part-time job at college or your first full-time position. Did you like your employer or did you despise them. If you are still in that job, would you work again in the same industry?

Would you change your industry and if so, why? PLEASE don't skip this process. By answering the questions, you will discover a way of escape from a job you hate and build a life that has meaning and purpose. Mark yourself overall on this exercise out of 10.

Chapter 2
The Staff

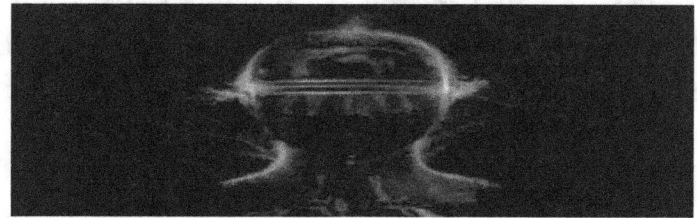

"If your actions inspire others to dream more, learn more, do more and become more, you are a leader." (John Quincy Adams) [7]

It is time to introduce you to the staff at the Abbey Hotel. The identity of past and current employees will be protected for the most part, although there are exceptions to this rule for which I make no apology.

So first up, Jack Danson, who was Senior Porter at the Abbey Hotel when I started.

---

[7] https://www.passiton.com/inspirational-quotes/6728-if-your-actions-inspire-others-to-dream-more

He was affectionately known as '*The Grapevine*' because he was usually the first to hear about all the breaking news and scandals in the Abbey Hotel.

So, what about the hotel porters? First up is the permanently chilled South American porter, Raul Gomez.

He was as relaxed as they come and liked to smoke e-cigarettes. When you meet Raul, the customary greeting is:

"Hey man."

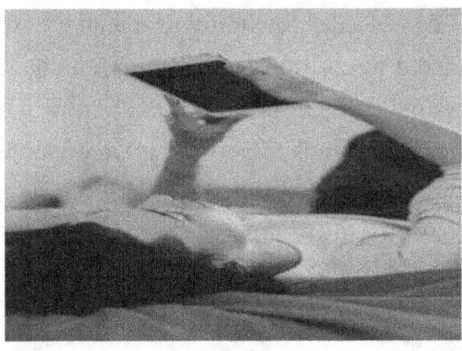

He started out as a day porter but eventually switched to nights. He saw less of the crazy Grealy family by night! Good for him. This guy has, in the past, had some odd jobs to perform for his employer, like driving Tom Grealy Senior and Adrian Grealy Senior to an Electric Light Orchestra concert in Dublin.

Raul recalls the story of Adrian Grealy and his father being completely out of their head with drink in the van on the way to Dublin. Sweet Jesus, only a chilled guy like Raul would put up with that shit. Talk about going the extra mile!

Sean *'Second Gear'* Shelton was a student at the time I started. He liked to chill on occasion with a cigarette in the toilets on the first floor of the hotel. Don't know what the guy was smoking, but he looked permanently comatose. Perhaps that's why his employer could fuck the head off him and it would go right over his head.

I think it's safe to say Shelton was built for comfort and not for speed! This guy will feature later in the story. Another student, Jack 'the joker' Johnston had an ability to take something serious in the hotel and cause us all to fall off the chair laughing. That said, he felt the wrath of my tongue when he came out with the ridiculous.

Marley *'Mad Dog'* Henson was a young porter. Mother of God, I couldn't repeat some of the things that came out of his mouth; otherwise my mother would disown me.

Let's just say Marley liked to party. Memories of *'Mad Dog'* taking a snooze in the toilet on the first floor for an hour after arriving into work and being completely hung over will stay with me for the rest of my life! Who could forget that story! I understand he left the Abbey Hotel last year. He got a better job. Not a hard thing to do! So thanks for the memories, *'Mad Dog'*.

And what about the receptionists?

They were a rather mixed bunch. Mary Bligh (Senior Receptionist), with over 30 years at the Abbey Hotel, was hard working. She deserves a knighthood for suffering the Grealys so long. That said, Mary Bligh may need counselling after she leaves the Abbey Hotel. A bit like marines returning from two tours of Afghanistan, they usually need counselling.

I decided to deal with the post-traumatic stress of working for the Grealys by suing them and publishing my memoirs.

One other notable and long-standing receptionist was Wilma, 'the witch' Henshaw.

Her manner was so aggressive that Adrian Grealy was afraid of her. Oh Jesus, was she scary! She reminded me of that mythical character Medusa.

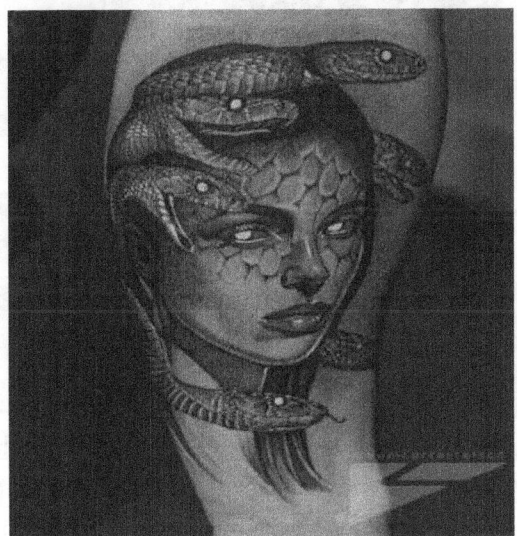

One look at Medusa and you would turn into stone. I mean one look from this receptionist would make a snowman melt and piss himself. She was a person in the mould of the Grealys. It is tragic to see somebody stay in their job even though it was clear she hated it.

Even Barney (played by Sylvester Stallone) in the *Expendables* wouldn't attempt a rescue mission if they knew Wilma was on duty. I think Barney would abort the mission and fly back home. Now that is saying something! Receptionists Betty Lynch and Elma Hansen were made to weep by Tom Grealy Junior.

And now I introduce you to chefs. Oh God, those lunatics! Chefs are renowned for their fiery temper. Several of them judged on their antics, appeared sex-starved! During my time, there were two head chefs. Zack Tyler was a brilliant head chef who lasted a year before he had enough of Tom Grealy Senior. The story goes that one day Zack Tyler was plating up food to go out to the restaurant when Tom Grealy Senior started removing garnish (lettuce in particular) from the plates. Tom believed that it was a waste of money. That was the straw that broke the camels' back for Zack Tyler. After Zack Tyler departed, 'Steady' Eddy O' Brien took over as head chef. Curtis Feinberg was a talented chef. He was second in command to Eddy O' Brien. We had a run-in (a sharp stand-off) in 2016. I will share more about that later. And not forgetting Jin (the charmer) Teck, from Malaysia. This guy met a bloody fate later so stay tuned.

And Ping Pong, another chef from Malaysia (also known as Durex) didn't last long.

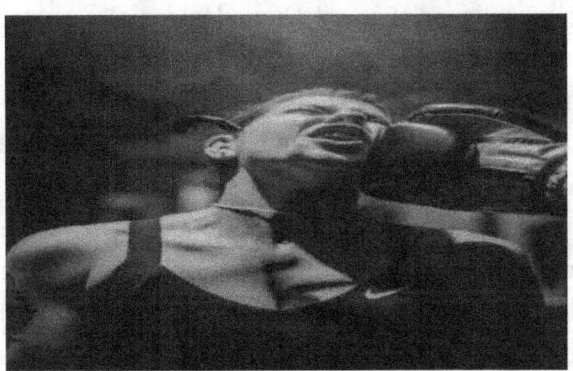

More about him later! Then there was Casey Dalton, a talented young chef who always made fresh breakfast for myself and Carl, 'the Cool' Carpenter. He recently finished his masters in culinary arts. This guy has a very bright future as a chef. I can't say enough good things about him. Gina

Ogden was a pastry chef at the with 30 years' experience at the Abbey Hotel whose hen-like pecking and fastidious nature did drive some of us mad!

fastidious	righteous	frugal	tidy	hoarding
perfectionism	obsessive			picky
control	compulsive			self-critical
stubbornness	personality			unemotional
orderliness	disorder			intellectual
rigid	detail orientation	focus	work	formality

<u>And what about the kitchen porters</u>? Brian Harley, who started out as a kitchen porter went on to qualify as a chef. He is now pursuing the path of becoming an electrician. Wishing this guy continued success! Harry Jenkins also started as a kitchen porter. Fortunately for him, early in 2018, he secured an apprenticeship as an airline mechanic at Dublin airport. Layla Wandsworth started out as a kitchen porter and then eventually ended up being restaurant supervisor. This lady is central to the plot. Tim 'Teapot' Timlin came in on a Friday evening at 4 pm and at 5 pm he was drinking tea with Jack Danson and Carl 'Cool' Carpenter. Although that has now changed since I left. I have a warning for pot washers. Don't do this job unless you want to end up having back surgery. Ask Tim Timlin!

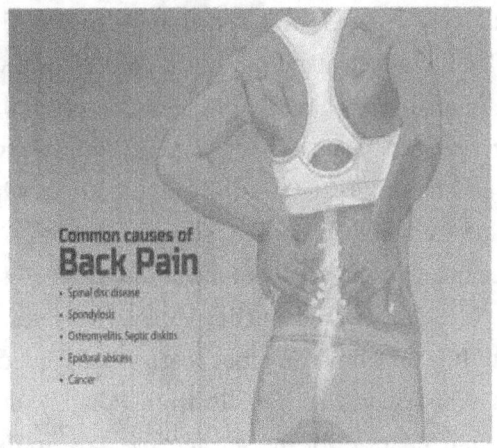

<u>And what about the restaurant staff</u>? Their job was extremely pressurised. Bill Benson, who was hired to replace Fanny Mae, walked out one Friday evening after he had enough of trying to figure out who was the boss. Was he to take orders from Tom Grealy Junior or Adrian Grealy or was it Tom Grealy Senior?

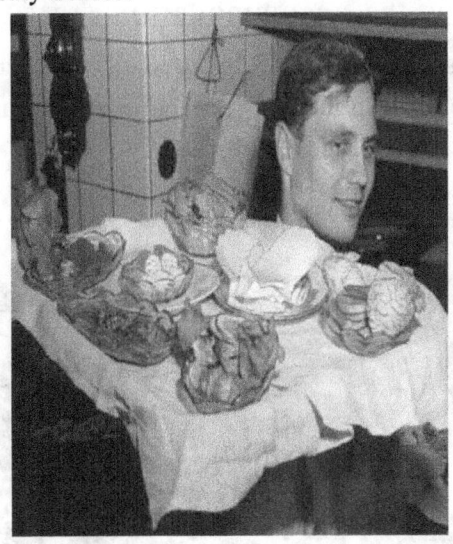

Brent Hayworth, who was restaurant manager, finally left in 2019. He literally walked out in the middle of a wedding! He had enough of Tom Grealy Junior. Brent was at the Abbey Hotel for nineteen years. That's a long time. He was hard working and had a great sense of humour. And what about Fanny Mae, another restaurant supervisor with 20 years' experience in the restaurant, who made the waitresses cry! For those of you who worked in the Abbey Hotel restaurant, I salute you. It takes immense grace to do what you guys do.

Layla Wandsworth (originally from Poland), deserves a special commendation for the service she gave to the Abbey Hotel. She is brave and speaks her truth. She endured bullying at the hands of Tom Grealy. To her husband Clint, thank you for all you support. Layla and her daughter will figure prominently in this book. Keep reading to hear about her explosive exit from the Abbey Hotel.

Next up is the accommodation staff

In my six years at the Abbey Hotel, they were on their fourth accommodation manager. That is a high turnover. At the time of my departure, Nancy Lawlor was the accommodation manager.

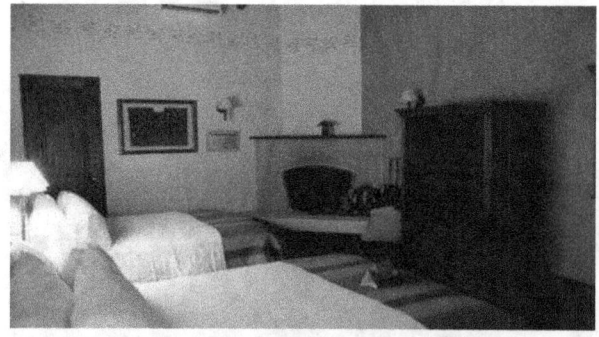

Greta Hepworth was responsible for booking rooms in the hotel and had twenty years' experience at the hotel and had also served as a wedding coordinator over the years.

The last time I saw Greta was that fateful day in August 2018 when I walked out of my job. It was the first time in six years that Greta spoke sharply to me. A short while thereafter, she left on sick leave due to stress. Apparently the culprit was Tom Grealy Junior. No surprise there!

When I arrived at the hotel in September 2012, there was no bar manager. However, in January 2013, a chap called William was hired as head barman. I really liked William!

However, he only lasted approximately twelve months. William was suspected by the Grealy family of stealing 10,000 euro, along with several kegs of beer. However, in the light of what I now know, this was not the case. The identity of the thieves is a mystery to this day.

Then along came a chap called Frank Alesworth a year later. He lasted a year! Tom Grealy Junior told him he simply wasn't doing his job. A case of the kettle calling the pot black! One year later Igor Bratislav was recruited as the bar manager. He figured out the bullshit environment quickly that existed in the Abbey Hotel and promptly left after twelve months and is now living in Australia.

The picture below tells the story of a high turnover of bar managers at the Abbey Hotel.

About one year later, Frank Alesworth returned. Frank was a henchman for Tom Grealy Junior as were others who could be easily manipulated. Tom Grealy Junior got other people to do his dirty work. And what about Lily Brackstone, with twenty years' service? This is a woman who confided in me that a few years before I joined the Abbey Hotel, that Tom Grealy Junior abused her verbally. She called her partner Kirk Rock to pick her up from work. She only returned to work after Mrs Grealy apologised on behalf of her mug of a son. Mrs Grealy had to beg Lily to return to work.

Special Mentions

Next up is Carl 'The Cool' Carpenter. I really liked this guy. He was the maintenance manager. He was a massive influence on getting me to record my first single, *'One More Chance' (*artist name – *Cathal J)*. It was Carl who coined the phrase *"All fur coat andno knickers,"* when referring to the reality of how the hotel was run. Essentially all style but no substance.

A special mention to May Hickson, who started out as a wages clerk, and went on to qualify as an accountant. Your level of professionalism was exceptional. Thank you May! May was replaced by Milly Bronte. Milly, your warm and infectious smile lifted everybody.

Thank you to Ciara on wash up. What many people don't know about Ciara is that she is a qualified chef. Hats off to you Ciara! And not forgetting the enigmatic electrician Sam Silk, who once told Anya Grealy to *"get rid of her two useless cunts of sons."* Priceless!

Scripture: *"Unless the Lord Build the House the work will be in vain."* (Psalm 127 v1)

Lesson: Because the Grealy family were not all singing from the same hymn sheet, it was impossible for the staff to strive for excellence. If the owners didn't care, why should the staff care? Wisdom and knowledge is what makes you stable in life. Make sure you have both of those attributes in abundance in life.

Exercise : Out of ten, how much would you say you like your current job?, If you can't answer seven out of ten, then it is time to start making plans to move on in the next 18 months at the latest.

Chapter 3
A Door of Hope

"Good manners will open doors that the best education cannot." (Clarence Thomas) [8]

The recession that gripped Ireland from 2007 to 2013 came as a shock to many. It left people struggling to keep basic bills paid. In August 2012, I sat in a dingy apartment with my wife, bemoaning my luck in life. I promised myself I would find a job and rebuild my life. My wife pointed to an advertisement in a local newspaper for a hotel porter at the Abbey Hotel in Roscommon town. I dusted down my curriculum. I thought, *"what have I to lose?"* A few weeks later, I got a call from a manager at the Abbey Hotel. He introduced himself as Adrian Grealy.

---

[8] https://www.brainyquote.com/quotes/clarence_thomas_137493

He asked me to turn up the following Tuesday at 6 pm. I went to the interview. I thought it went well and was feeling confident that I was going to get the job. I got a phone call from Adrian Grealy saying that I didn't get the job. He said "The one thing that prevented me from getting the job was that I was living too far away." I was gutted.

But surprisingly, the following week I got a phone call from Adrian Grealy. He said that the job was mine as the guy who got offered the job didn't accept the job offer. I was obviously delighted. Up until that point, I was getting bits of painting work, delivering catalogues and selling milk. I started work the next day. I was shown around and got a quick induction by Jack Danson (Senior Day Porter). I was also made very welcome by "Steady" Eddy O' Brien when he met me at the door and said, "Welcome to Hell."

What he didn't realise was that a chap in the spirit of John the Baptist just walked through the door. Yah, hell was about to get its ass kicked. And that's the end of chapter 3. Time for some spiritual nourishment! Congratulations for getting to the end of chapter 3.

Scripture: *"I will return her vineyards to her and transform the Valley of Trouble into a (gateway) door of hope in the valley of death."* (Hosea 2 v 15)

Lesson: When the opportunity to work at the Abbey Hotel came up, I jumped at it. It signalled a new beginning. At that time in my life, I was separated from my wife and had other personal challenges. You don't have to stay in that shitty dead-end job forever.

Change begins with you making a decision to change and then following through. Remember in the valley of trouble, God will open a door of hope!

Exercise: What are you willing to do to change your job? If you are will to spend 10,000 euro in the next five years to retrain and get better paid in a job that you would love THEN I know you are SERIOUS. That is the litmus test. Out of ten, how determined and how serious are you about getting out of that dead-end job.

Chapter 4
Wolves in Sheep's Clothing

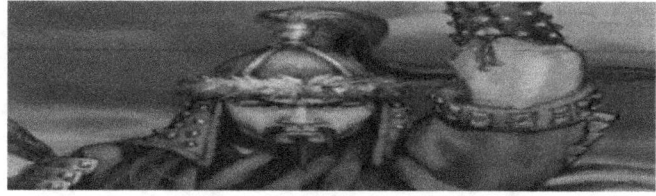

"The Tausennennigan Ob'nn warlords look like cuddly 'teddy-bears'? Yes, they do, and they would cheerfully exterminate your entire race for making that observation!"[9]

My first bruising account with Adrian Grealy was eight weeks into my tenure at the Abbey Hotel. One night, there was a business meeting in the Crofton suite for approximately twenty people. All meetings, events and restaurant bookings are up on a board in the kitchen for all the staff to see. When looking at a meeting, porters need to ascertain if there are refreshments being served to the client. When I looked at the

---

[9] Howard Taylor, "Schlock Mercenary the Tub of Happiness" (The Tayler Corporation, 2007)

board, I *thought* I saw the initials "tbc", which means 'to be confirmed'. Simply put, it will be confirmed by the client if they need tea and coffee. I had misread the board. Oh crap!

The board actually read "tcb" which is short-hand for tea, coffee and biscuits. Twenty minutes later, Adrian Grealy came storming in with a rage and a satanic fury, the likes of which I had never seen before in the workplace. I was informed of the mistake in a very aggressive manner. I promptly rectified the matter.

Tea, coffee and biscuits were served to the Crofton suite within twenty minutes. As soon as the matter was rectified, Adrian Greely asked me to come into the ballroom. There, he proceeded to verbally abuse me. It was *"fucking sloppy and unacceptable,"* in his words. Not exactly the vocabulary used by management in the 21st century.

To say that I was shaken was an understatement. The last time an employer spoke to me like that; I promptly told them to fuck off and ended my employment. I was so shaken by the verbal abuse that I took four days off work. When I returned to work, Adrian Grealy had a letter from me on his desk. We went into the foyer and spoke. Adrian Greely apologised for the way he spoke to me. He said the next time

I was upset, "I shouldn't write a letter but rather take my anger out on a punch bag." The guy is fortunate that in the six years I worked at the Abbey Hotel, I didn't punch him! This is a guy who routinely subjected his father to elder abuse by shouting and screaming at him in the presence of staff.

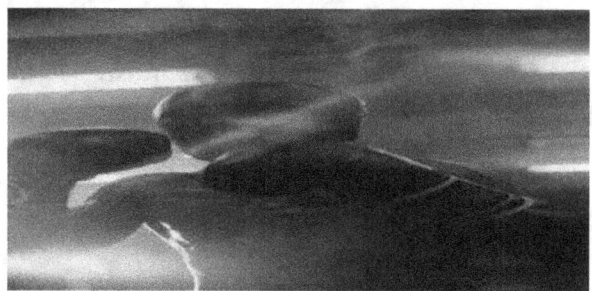

Jesus declared *"Beware of false prophets who come to you in sheep's clothing, but inwardly they are ravenous wolves. Do men gather grapes of thorns, or figs of thistles? Even so every good tree bears forth good fruit but a corrupt tree brings forth bad fruit. A good tree cannot bear bad fruit; neither can a corrupt tree bear good fruit. Every tree that that doesn't bear good fruit will be cut down and cast into the fire. <u>You shall know them by their fruits</u>."* [10]

When you are trying to rebuild your life in the middle of a recession, you keep taking shit from these people. You turn the other cheek. You keep telling yourself you will be gone in one year and you say the same thing again next year. It is the fear of change that keeps you stuck in a rut.

---

[10] Matthew 7:19-20 (The Bible)

You know that they are breaking the rules of all human decency. You know in your heart that these people are complete and utter madmen.

One last story to finish off this chapter. The story relates to Kayla Patova, who worked on wash-up at the Abbey Hotel. Adrian Grealy had paid her husband to install a satellite system at his home. Shortly thereafter, Adrian Grealy changed his mind about the installation of the TV/satellite system. He had the satellite system uninstalled and asked for a refund from Kayla's husband. Adrian Grealy made it clear that if he wasn't refunded, he would have the Abbey Hotel garnish the money from her wages at the Abbey Hotel. The source of this story is from the son of a prominent businessman in my hometown. The prophet Ezekiel described these types of leaders as false shepherds; Ezekiel 34 v 3 *"You drink the milk, wear the wool and butcher the best animals, but you let your flocks starve."*

It is for people like Kayla that I write this book. I have no doubt that this book is being used to restore the dignity of many past and present employees of the Abbey Hotel.

Scripture: *"Let Love be without hypocrisy."* (Romans 12 v 9)

Lesson: Do not be fooled by person's appearance. Only be ever impressed by their character.

Exercise: How many times has an employer or fellow worker treated you disrespectfully in the last twelve months? Once, twice, three times?

Chapter 5
A Dirty Little Secret

"The bully in the office hinders the morale, teamwork, productivity and well-being of others who actually want and enjoy all of the above." [11]

While this book is a collection of my memoirs as a hotel porter at the Abbey Hotel, Roscommon, its goal is to deal with the scourge, the shame and one of Ireland's dirty and hidden secrets in the workplace; bullying. In the *Maurice Mc Cabe*

---
[11] (Ty Howard) www.tyquotes.com

case, an Irish police officer, who exposed corruption at the highest level in Ireland's police force; was a victim of bullying by his employer. I share this brief note on the Mc Cabe case to explain to you how his insidious spirit works to destroy lives. [12]

Bullying and sexual harassment of female members of staff was a regular part of life at the Abbey Hotel. It was considered normal and part of the hotel culture. Nobody dared to speak out against the bullying in the Abbey. I guess most people like the quiet life.

So just who is a bully and what are the characteristics of a bully? Studies show that bullies lack pro-social behaviour.

The worst of bullies usually have strained relationships with parents and peers. Bullies seek out their victims; usually those who are non-assertive and have low self-esteem. Experts believe the way to deal with a bully is a) to walk away and b) to have a friend close by.

Bullies won't run the risk of attacking a vulnerable person if they are in a group. [13]Indeed, the Bar Council of Ireland has just revealed the results of a survey taken by 567 men and women out of its 2,000 members. *"Discrimination, sexual harassment and bullying were seen as widespread amongst members. But it found that the vast majority did not report such incidents because it was perceived as commonplace or acceptable or because of a fear of repercussions."* This was the same in the Abbey Hotel. It was considered normal.

---

[12] https://www.irishtimes.com/news/crime-and-law/maurice-mccabe-settles-high-court

[13] https://psychologytoday.com

It is quite shocking and yet unsurprising in Irish society when even this type of gross and disgusting behaviour is tolerated by practicing barristers in this jurisdiction. [14]

At my second hearing at the Work Place Relations Commission, a former employee was able to share her experience of bullying at the hands of Tom Grealy Junior. That person was Layla Wandsworth. I hope that by Layla sharing her story at the WRC of an abusive employer, other people will step forward and be set free from their fears and face the monster that is bullying. It is only when we bring these dark and hidden things of shame into the light can employees begin to recover and heal.

While the legislation is there to empower people, most are unwilling to go to court. They would rather move on from the trauma imposed by a former employer and start afresh. It goes without saying that legal proceedings against an employer are

---

[14] Orla O' Donnell, legal affairs correspondent at RTE (10th Oct 2019) https://www.rte.ie/news/ireland/2019/1010/1082371-bar-council-survey/?fbclid

quite traumatic and most employers will simply deny all wrongdoing. For most employees, the fear of losing a legal battle weighs heavily on employees' minds when considering whether they should take legal action against their employer. Many won't take that risk as generally the loser will pay legal costs for both sides if it goes beyond the Workplace Relations Commission stage. Many families have mortgages and simply won't run the risk of losing their home.

For those of you considering taking legal action against an employer; there are a range of options out there. There is ample information available at the Citizens Advice Bureau. Also, the WRC have a mediation service available if an employee believes the relationship between employee and employer can be saved.

For employers, the old adage of 'prevention is better than cure' is so true. Invest in your employees' welfare and I assure you that the risk of being sued by an employee will be reduced substantially.

Scripture: *"For God has not given us the Spirit of fear but of power, love and a sound mind."* (2 Timothy 1 v 7)

Lesson: Please learn to value yourself. Stand up to bullies. You are made in the image of God. If people have demeaned you in the past and stripped you of your dignity, allow God's grace to restore you and become courageous once more. Boldness does not drop on you, it grows on you. Ask yourself, how I can be bold and assertive? Forget bullshit assertiveness courses. They don't work! Boldness comes from developing character.

Exercise: <u>Meditate</u> on the above scripture ONLY for the next 90 days and then see if your boldness levels increase. Just do it. After 90 days, mark yourself out of ten in terms of an increase in boldness.

Chapter 6
A Hidden Epidemic

Recent Studies have shown that workplace bullying is on the rise. [15]Research has proven that almost 75% of employees surveyed had been affected by workplace bullying.[16] The 2017 US workplace Bullying Survey showed that almost 60% US workers are affected by it. [17]It has also been shown that although workplace bullying is *"not equally split between men (70%) and women (30%), women tend to bully more women than men (more than 65% in both cases)."*

---

[15] .https://www.acas.org.uk/stress-and-anxiety-at-work

[16] http://www.workplacebullying.org/multi/img/2017/Infographic-2017.png

[17] http://www.workplaceviolence911.com/docs/20081215.pdf

Studies have also shown that workplace bullying is also not carried out by the supervisors and superiors alone, but also by co-workers. In all cases, it is a *'form of power struggle'*. [18]An Australian study found that almost one in two Australians will face some kind of workplace bullying in their lifetime. Of those bullied, 40 per cent of people experienced workplace bullying. [19]

Research also shows that bullying at work is a contributing factor to suicides. [20]A 2011 survey by UNISON supports these findings with 60% from 6,000 respondents reporting either experiencing or witnessing bullying in their job. [21]Additionally, in a report released in November 2015, the 'Acas' (in the UK) revealed that their helpline received 20,000 phone calls in relation to bullying. [22]

---

[18] Hodson, Randy & Roscigno, V. & Lopez, Steven. (2006). "Chaos and the Abuse of Power: Workplace Bullying in Organisational and Interactional Context. Workplace Bullying in Organisational and Interactional Context"

[19] https://www.abc.net.au/news/2016-10-09/half-all-australians-experience-workplace-bullying-survey-finds/7916230

[20]. https://www.forbes.com/sites/pragyaagarwaleurope/2018/07/29/workplace-bullying-here-is-why-we-need-to-talk-about-bullying-in-the-work-place/#68cbd5cc3259

[21] https://www.unison.org.uk/content/uploads/2013/07/On-line-Catalogue216953.pdf

[22] https://www.acas.org.uk/seeking-better-solutions-tackling-bullying-and-ill-treatment-in-britains-workplaces

Scripture: *"Do not fear or be in dread of them, for it is the LORD your God who goes with you. He will not leave you or forsake you."* (Deuteronomy 31 v 6).

Lesson: Don't be an asshole. Be a decent human being, especially at work.

Exercise: Out of a mark of ten, how likely are you to share information from this book.

Part 2
Verdict please

Chapter 7
A Legal Perspective

"Knowledge is power, information is liberating. Education is the premise of progress, in every society, in every family." [23]

Ireland has come a long way in terms of developing a plethora of legislation which protects workers' rights and their dignity at work. The playing field between employer and employee is slowly being levelled, although that said causation is still the biggest obstacle to overcome as seen in *Berber v Dunne*.[24] Please don't skip this bit. Know the law in this jurisdiction on bullying! Bullying is "...*repeated and*

---

[23] Kofi Annan, United Nations Press Release, SG/SM/6268 (23rd. June 1997)

[24] Berber v Dunne's Stores Ltd (2009) ELR 61.

inappropriate behaviour, direct or indirect, whether verbal, physical or otherwise, conducted by one or more persons against another or others, at the place of work, and/or in the course of employment, which could reasonably be regarded as undermining the individual's right to dignity at work. An isolated incident of the behaviour described in this definition may be an affront to dignity at work, as a once off incident, is not considered to be bullying."[25]

In *Ruffley v The Board of Management of St. Anne's School*[26] the Supreme Court shone a light on the key elements on the test for bullying focussing on the fundamental boxes to be ticked to trigger a claim for damages.

The conduct should be:

i. Repeated

> The court emphasised the requirement for conduct to be repeated in order to progress in the test. Bullying requires "A pattern of behaviour, not a number of incidences," not 'merely wrong' i.e. does not need to be unlawful or erroneous behaviour. [27]

---

[25] HSA Code of practice on Bullying 2007, adopted by the Supreme Court in Quigley v Complex Tooling & Mouldings {2008} IESC 44

[26] Anne Ruffley v St Anne's Board of Management, {2008} IEHC 235 and Supreme court record number 2016/24

[27] https://bnsolicitors.ie/una-ruffley-v-board-management-st-annes-school/

ii. Amount to Inappropriate Behaviour

The Supreme Court defined inappropriate behaviour as that which is inappropriate at a *"human level"* and held that *"the test looks to the question of propriety in human relations"*. [28]

iii. Undermine the Employees Dignity at Work

The Supreme Court held that this was a separate, distinct and important component of the bullying definition *"which limits the claims which may be made to those which may be described as outrageous, unacceptable and exceeding all bounds tolerated by decent society."* The Supreme Court made it clear that the conduct which will qualify as undermining of an individual's right to dignity at work must be *"both severe and normally offensive at a human level."* [29]

Let's look at the three constituent elements of this test. The first test of bullying is that there must be repeated bullying over a sustained period of time. There must be a pattern. At the Abbey Hotel, I and countless employees experienced bullying over a sustained period of time. With regard to the second leg of the test, the behaviour must be inappropriate.

---

[28] ibid 25

[29] https://www.algoodbody.com/insights-publications/workplace-bullying-significant-supreme-court-decision-clarifying-the-positi

Well let me give you a few examples of inappropriate behaviour. Adrian Grealy had a habit of making porters work shitty hours (working 10/11 hr. shifts that would finish at midnight) or reducing their hours if he felt your performance wasn't up to scratch.

Tom Grealy Junior also tried this tactic on me shortly before I left! He had Jack Danson reduce my hours. And finally the third leg of the test, dignity at work. The behaviour must be "severe and offensive at a human level." Let me give you just one example of "severe and offensive" behaviour at a human level." [30]

During my time at the Abbey Hotel, we had an obnoxious wedding coordinator by the name of Kelly Brixton. Tom Grealy Junior thought the sun shone out of her arse. Ms Brixton was hired as a wedding coordinator in March 2016. She felt this entitled her to run around the hotel and be another shitty enforcer for her dictator boss, Tom Grealy Junior.

---

[30] ibid 27

In October 2016 there was an incident that happened between me and Kelly Brixton that would make it clear to her that I was one of those people who tolerated fools. One morning in October 2016, I took a call from my wife. She seemed rather distressed. As I took the call, Kelly Brixton told me to get off the phone. I must tell you that I had the phone on loudspeaker. I proceeded to tell Kelly Brixton to *"Fuck off."*

Waitresses Maria Kosovo and Inga Hilbert were present to witness this incident. However, worse was to come. Early in 2017, during preparation for the wedding, Kelly Brixton threw a bunch of tacks at me in the reception area of the hotel. That was the final straw. I spoke with Mrs Grealy about this. Kelly Brixton left the hotel six months later. What is shocking is that the Abbey Hotel did not inform employees that there was an employment handbook which explained the consequences for bullying, intimidation, harassment and sexual harassment.

The employees of the Abbey Hotel were essentially kept in the dark and disempowered as employees. The employees of the Abbey Hotel lived in fear of bringing complaints against Adrian Grealy or Tom Grealy.

How about this for a scary incident! In January 2016, Donald J Trump was elected the 45th president of the United States. I made no secret of my prayer that he would be elected president of the United States. This obviously pissed off a certain group of people in the Abbey Hotel. One of those people was Curtis Feinberg. This guy started a conversation with me about Donald Trump.

He asked me what I thought about Donald Trump. I replied, "Donald Trump is the president of the United States and he can pretty much do what he wants." To make a long story short, Curtis Feinberg, with a kitchen knife in his hand, went toe to toe with me. I looked Curtis Feinberg in the eye and told him that if he started something he should finish it. Zack Tyler was a witness to these events.

Scripture: *"My people are destroyed for lack of knowledge."* (Hosea 4 v 6)

Lesson: The above scripture encapsulates what not only happened at the Abbey Hotel but happens every day in workplaces around Ireland. I strongly suggest to both employees and employers to know what the law is. Employers, get your house in order.

Exercise: In the next three months, read the Irish Constitution. It is actually quite a short read. Then answer the question; out of ten, how inspired are you to learn more about law in your area of employment?

Chapter 8
Tick-Box Exercises

"Just because something isn't a lie does not mean it is not deceptive. A liar knows that he is a liar, but one who speaks mere portions of truth in order to deceive is a craftsman of destruction." (Criss Jami) [31]

---

[31] Criss Jami (lead singer of the rock band Venus)
https://www.goodreads.com/quotes/463916-just-because-something-isn-t-a-lie-does-not-mean-that

In order for you to understand how the Grealy family got away with so much for so long, you need to understand that the Abbey Hotel have operated for decades outside of the law in the area of 'bullying their employees'. They have duped and deceived their employees by keeping them in the dark.

Real employers keep their employees informed and empower them to become better at their job. The Grealy family understood that if they can keep employees ignorant, they would, in the words of the prophet Hosea, be *'destroyed for lack of knowledge'*. Gandhi understood this when he said that a people who are *"wise and knowledgeable cannot be exploited."* This employee handbook was hidden from employees! Shocking but true!

(A) <u>Now read the Abbey Hotels definition of bullying</u>

Even if you were one of the fortunate employees who got their hands on the employee handbook you would have scratched your head and said *"what the fuck is this, are these guys for real."* One must bear in mind that Shelton Healy (the financial controller) thinks he got this on the Internet. It WASN'T drafted by a lawyer. Shock horror, yes, I know! So let's look at what the employee handbook says about bullying. *"Bullying is repeated inappropriate behaviour directed at an individual or group of people, to their face or behind their back, which undermines a person's right to dignity at work."*

<u>Let us take one point from the statement and examine it!</u>

Tom Grealy, repeatedly demeaned employees behind their back. How do I know this? Well because I have testimonies from many Abbey Hotel staff to that effect.

The Abbey Hotel's definition of bullying goes on to state that *"Bullying may be verbal, physical or both and may involve any number of people and that bullying is most easily recognised because the action is reasonably seen as cruel, hostile or aggressive, intimidating, and/or degrading."*

Tom Grealy once confided in me that he and I were way above guys like Bratislav who was a kitchen porter. He was quite graphic about this. <u>He pointed to the floor</u> indicating that this was the status that Bratislav had in his eyes. This is a guy who went about systematically and covertly denigrating the staff. How can I describe this guy?

Can I borrow a phrase from the movie *'Tango and Cash'* to describe Tom Grealy Junior? "FUBAR-FUCKED UP BEYOND ALL RECOGNITION."

He saw the employees at the Abbey Hotel as slaves. Well, I have a newsflash for Tom Grealy Junior; the illusion that he is Lord of the manor is over.

(B) <u>Too little too late</u>!

After I left the Abbey Hotel in August 2108, my former employer came up with the genius idea of hiring a human resource manager. All employees now have a 103 page human resource manual. Another tick box exercise? Probably! As they say in Roscommon, *"it's a bit late when the horse has bolted."* How moronic! Hypocrisy on a grand level.

Scripture: *"But test everything, hold fast to what is good."* (1 Thessalonians 5 v 21)

Lesson: Failure to be authentic in life will ensure that sooner or later, you will be exposed as a fraud. Strive to be genuine in everything that you do in life. Being genuine will cause others to trust you while being disingenuous will cause you to be held up to the light and exposed as a fool.

Exercise: Another question! Out of ten, how authentic do you think you are as a person?

Chapter 9
Harassment (including sexual harassment)

(A) The Employment Equality Acts 1998-2015

This piece of legislation places an obligation on all employers to prevent harassment in the workplace. Under this law, you are entitled to bring a claim to the Workplace Relations Commission and your employer may be obliged to pay you compensation if you are harassed by reason of your:

- "Gender
- Civil Status
- Family status, for example, as a parent of a child
- Sexual orientation
- Age
- Disability
- Race
- Religious belief
- Membership of traveller community"

Harassment based on any of the above grounds is a form of discrimination in relation to conditions of employment. Some examples could include making jokes or derogatory comments. The Employment Equality Acts 1998-2015 defines harassment as *'unwanted conduct'* which is related to any of the nine discriminatory grounds above.

Sexual harassment is any form of *"unwanted verbal, non-verbal or physical conduct of a sexual nature."* Some examples include unwanted physical contact or unwelcome propositions. In both cases, it is identified as a conduct which "has the purpose of effect of violating a person's dignity and creating a hostile, degrading, humiliating or offensive environment for the person" and it is prohibited.

The "unwanted conduct" includes:

- Spoken words
- Gestures – (including offensive gestures or facial expressions)
- Production and display of written words, pictures and other material (unwelcome emails or other offensive material)

Harassment or sexual harassment can be by a co-worker, your boss or someone in a superior position, a client, a customer or any other business contact. It can take place at work or on a training course, or on a work trip, at a work or social event or any other occasion connected with your job.[32]

(B) <u>Hotels definition of harassment as of August 2012</u>

"As with bullying, harassment is any act or conduct, including spoken words, gestures or the production, display or circulation of written words, pictures or other material if

---

[32]https://www.ihrec.ie/app/uploads/download/pdf/code_of_practice_on_sexual_harassment_and_harassment.pdf

the action or conduct is unwelcome to the employee and could reasonably be regarded as being offensive, humiliating or intimidating. Repeated harassment could <u>easily</u> be regarded as bullying."

<u>As hotel porters,</u> we were required to carry a phone so that all departments could liaise with us. However, the level of phone calls porters had to take and the abuse that came from certain receptionists was completely disproportionate to what should be considered reasonable in the hotel industry. Layla Wandsworth shared her own story with me of the brutal reality and hell she endured. She was continually pestered on her days off by Tom Grealy Junior to come in and cover. Layla had no problem covering for staff members if it was reasonable to do so. However, she was always the one singled out for this duty. Things had gotten so bad that it nearly wrecked her marriage and mental health.

The Abbey hotels policy on harassment and bullying states that the following list, although not exhaustive, could violate this policy. They were as follows: *"personal insults and name calling, unjustified personal contact, sarcasm, shouting (in public or in private), sneering, instantaneous rage often over trivial issues, setting someone up for failure, undermining someone's work or job performance, withholding critical information to cause extreme embarrassment or failure, aggression, ignoring or neglecting someone as an act of cruelty, continuously refusing reasonable requests, meanness or aggression, intimidation and threats in general and undermining someone's work or job performance."*

Now I am going to share Layla Wandsworth's dramatic departure from the Abbey Hotel. It was late in 2017. In March 2017, she had booked her holidays for the month of August. It was a special holiday as it included a wedding in her native Poland. However, Tom Grealy Junior wanted her back two days earlier than the date on the holiday request that he had signed off in March. That meant Layla and her husband had to reschedule their return flight, which cost her an extra 110 euros. Layla returned back to work from her holidays, stressed. Several days later, she collapsed in the restaurant and was unconscious. NOBODY at the Abbey Hotel called 999.

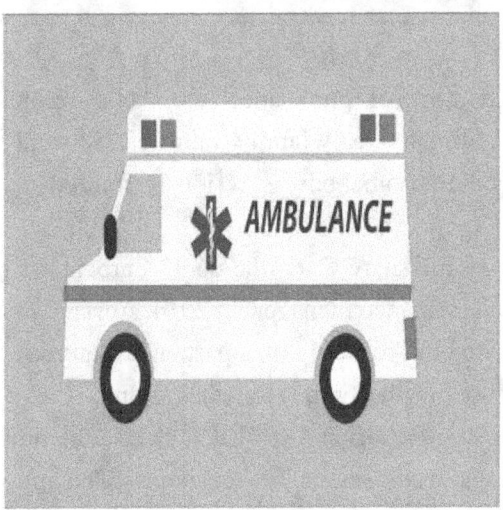

Her husband had to call 999 and take her to the hospital. Layla was traumatised by what happened and had to go on sick leave. This incident depicts the utter depravity of Tom Grealy Junior and the lack of duty of care that he demonstrated toward the staff at the Abbey Hotel.

At the time of publication the Abbey Hotel has re-opened. With the Grealy family running it, it is only a matter of time before somebody is seriously injured or commits suicide.

Now let me share Carl "the cool" Carpenter's story. He was the maintenance manager. In 2014, Adrian Grealy asked Carl Carpenter if he would, on a particular Saturday morning, assemble some play items for his children. Carl Carpenter made it clear to Adrian Grealy that if he had time on that Saturday he would assemble the items. One must bear in mind that Carl Carpenter was not contracted to work Saturdays. In any event, this would have been a favour! Carl Carpenter only worked three days a week. He returned the following Wednesday to work. He was met by a furious and outraged Adrian Grealy. Adrian made it clear that he was outraged that Carl had not come to Adrian's home to assemble the toys for his kids. Adrian was of the understanding that Carl had promised to assemble the toys. Adrian and Carl went toe to toe in the foyer of the hotel. Carl freely confided in me that it was a miracle it didn't come to blows!

(C) <u>Sexual harassment at the Abbey Hotel</u>

I am now going to deal with the issue of sexual harassment. Layla Wandsworth and her daughter, Miranda, were the victims of sexual harassment in 2013 and 2014. Before I go into their story let's look at what the Abbey Hotels handbook on sexual harassment had to say.

Examples of sexual harassment may include:

- *"Gestures with sexual meaning or connotation*
- *Displaying sexually suggestive objects, pictures, calendars*
- *Sending suggestive and pornographic correspondence including faxes, text messages or e-mails*

- *Unwelcome sexual comments and jokes*
- *Unwelcome physical conduct such as pinching, unnecessary touching, etc."*

For the lads at the Abbey Hotel, you were sexually harassing women even if you didn't know this was sexual harassment!

Oh that's right; you didn't get an employee handbook. And for those of you who did, you probably put a match to it after your first week at the Abbey Hotel. By now, guys, your human resource manager, Matilda, has explained the legal definition of sexual harassment. At least I hope she has.

Now let's deal with the first incident of sexual harassment that I became aware of during my six years at the Abbey. It concerned Layla Wandsworth who started out as a kitchen porter, qualified as a chef and eventually became a restaurant supervisor. Her testimony at my second Workplace Relations Commission was truly powerful.

She explained how many times she was alone in the hotel with the morning chef. It came to a point in 2013 where she was sexually harassed by Jin Tech, a Malaysian chef. She had experienced this many times at the Abbey Hotel. It was so awful that Layla immediately called her husband.

Her husband came and assaulted Jin Tech. Jin Tech was released from his contract at the Abbey Hotel the next day.

What is fascinating about the assault is that Layla's husband went to the police station and freely admitted that he assaulted Jin Tech. The police refused to arrest him. They stated that they couldn't arrest him unless the Abbey Hotel made a complaint. The police refused to arrest him.

The police were aware that Jin Tech had previously sexually harassed a young lady in a nightclub. This is a shocking trauma for a female member of staff at the Abbey Hotel to endure in broad daylight.

There was no record of this in the Abbey Hotel's incident book because the Abbey Hotel didn't have an incident book!

This incident was followed by sexual harassment of her daughter, Kristine, in early 2014. The harassment was carried out on her by another chef, Ping Pong, otherwise known as Durex by his colleagues.

This was not a one-off incident. Her dad came steaming into the hotel. Ping Pong was immediately fired. The Abbey Hotel employee handbook states that "employees should never accept bullying, harassment or sexual harassment but should work to stop it or report it."

And hey what about this beautiful line; *"It is the hotel's responsibility to make sure employees are not afraid to ask for assistance, raise a grievance or make a complaint."* The problem was that the staff were *afraid (terrified)* to make a complaint to the Grealy family. Now for some spiritual nourishment after reading that difficult chapter!

Scripture: *"Let there be no filthiness nor crude joking, which are out of place, but instead let there be thanksgiving."* (Ephesians 5 v 4)

Lesson: For those of you chaps who somehow think cracking crude jokes makes you a man, I assure you it doesn't. It makes you an idiot. Respect your co-worker. Learn to respect boundaries in relationships.

Exercise: For the guys I have a question; out of ten, how do you rate the language that comes out of your mouth in relation to women (particularly at work).

Chapter 10
Fair Procedures

"Justice must be rooted in confidence and confidence is destroyed when right minded people go away thinking: the judge was biased (as per Lord Denning)" [33]

Twin pillars of Fair procedures

There are two principles that are considered to be the bedrock of fair procedures in law in this jurisdiction. The first

---

[33] Metropolitan Properties Co (FGC) Ltd v Lannon {1968} 3 All ER 304

is *Audi alteram partem* (both sides must be heard). The court in *Kielty v Minister for Social Welfare* [34] stated that *"Natural justice is not observed if the scales of justice are tilted against one side all through the proceedings. Audi Alteram Partem means both sides must be fairly heard. That is not done if one party is allowed to send in his evidence in writing, free from the truth eliciting processes of a confrontation which are inherent in an oral hearing, whilst his opponent is compelled to run the gauntlet or oral examination and cross-examination. The dispensation* of *justice must be even handed in form as well as in content."*

So how does this apply to the Abbey Hotel? Well for a start, there were no proper disciplinary procedures in place. At my hearing against the Abbey Hotel at the WRC, Anya Grealy stated that in the past, they have used the services of a human resource management consultancy firm when seeking to construct and keep their disciplinary grievance procedures in check. I would love to know who that cowboy outfit is.

The second principle upon which fair procedures is built on is the Latin maxim, *'nemo iudex in causa sua'*, reflects the principle of natural justice that no-one should be a judge in their own cause. [35] Tom Grealy was going to be the judge in his own case. In fact he was the judge. He stated that neither he nor the Abbey Hotel had done any wrong! The level of

---

[34] Kielty v Minister for Social Welfare No 2 (1977) IR 267

[35] Orange Communications v Director of Communications (N0 2) {2000} 4 I.R 159 at p221

arrogance that this guy exhibited is the equivalent of putting two fingers up to the legislature. This hotel operated as if it was above the law. But like the *'Untouchables'* movie, starring Sean Connery, Al Capone got found out by an accountant!

Let's look at the Complaints procedure at the Abbey Hotels (horse manure!) on the next page

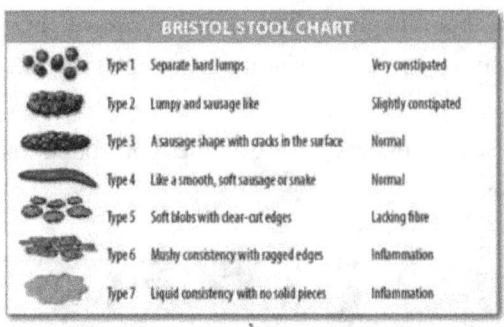

It states anyone who believes they are experiencing inappropriate behaviour should refer to the 'Code of Practice Detailing Procedures for addressing Bullying in the Workplace'. *Most employees were never aware that such thing as an employment handbook existed and if* they did knew that it existed, they certainly didn't read it.

There was no training on key topics such as *'dignity at work'*. I only found out about this employee handbook when I was preparing a project for employment law at Athlone Institute of Technology in January 2017. The truth of the matter is that this handbook was a sham and basically a tick box exercise.

The Code also states that the Hotel will <u>identify and train selected staff to act as contact persons</u>. In reality, there was nobody trained or selected to deal with these matters.

Nobody really knew who to go to because nobody was nominated (except management) in the employment handbook. I assure you that 'management' was a very vague term in the Abbey Hotel because there were '*more chiefs than Indians*' running around that hotel!

Furthermore, the code states that "*all questions and complaints will be taken seriously, treated confidentially and addressed as soon as practicable. The hotel will work to safeguard staff from innuendo and harmful gossip related to complaints.*" The truth is that there were no proper HR procedures in place to document and record issues that employees encountered. A wise man once said, *"No society wants you to become wise, it is against the investment of all societies. If people are wise, they cannot be exploited, it they are wise they cannot be subjugated, they cannot be forced into a mechanical life to live like a robot."* [36]

Special requirements for managers

In relation to managers, the Abbey Hotel's policy stated that *"anyone in a position of authority has a responsibility to act if they witness any misconduct or inappropriate behaviour and that a complaint is not required to address an obvious violation of hotel policy."*

---

[36] www.osho.com

This has got to be one of the most <u>misleading</u>, hypocritical and poorly drafted documents any employment lawyer will ever lay his eyes on. It also states that *"failing to act may make a person in a position of authority responsible for that issue or for continued related issues."*

This document was not drafted by a lawyer but *"was found on the internet"* according to the financial controller of the Abbey Hotel when I asked him in January 2018 about the source of the document. The picture below of a donkey head encapsulates my thoughts on the matter.

Disciplinary Procedures

The Abbey Hotel's employee handbook stated that *"disciplinary issues within the Hotel will be dealt with in a 'fair and impartial manner' consistent with the national Code of Practice."* Really, if that was the case, why did they hire a full time human resource manager after I left?

Read this buffoon of a statement from the Abbey Hotel's employee handbook, *"Basic <u>responsibility for the maintenance of discipline lies with the individual employee</u>."* Sounds like an enterprise where the employer is on permanent vacation in the Bahamas and YOU, the employee get to run the ship! <u>Have you ever</u> read such a diabolic statement in the midst of an employment document?

This is a classic example of an employer abdicating complete and utter responsibility for discipline at the Abbey Hotel. Statements like this explain the toxic, chaotic, dysfunctional and insane environment that was the Abbey Hotel. It was akin to The Muppet show!

The handbook further states that *"employees are entitled to be given a fair hearing before any disciplinary decision is taken against them."*

Read this complete utter load of tripe as to how employees will be treated DIFFERENTLY based on the merits of the case, *"The Hotel reserves the right to treat each situation independently based solely on the merits of the case and taking into account the unique considerations that may apply to the individual(s) involved."*

So the Abbey Hotel, it seems, will not base their decisions when implementing disciplinary procedures on facts or indeed objective criteria but on 'the merits of the case'. This was the case with Layla Wandsworth, who, when applying for holiday leave, was discriminated against. Other employees were treated more favourably.

Important procedures

Read this load of rubbish and then I will pick through it.

"Procedures are necessary to ensure discipline is maintained in the workplace by applying corrective actions in a fair and consistent manner and by ensuring grievances are handled in accordance with the principles of natural justice and fairness."

"<u>These procedures serve a dual purpose</u>:

- *They provide a framework that enables management to maintain satisfactory standards for a safe, effective and efficient business and*
- *They form a process whereby alleged failures by an employee to comply with these standards may be fairly and sensitively addressed.*

The procedures will be explained to employees at the commencement of employment and will be included in induction and occasional refresher training." OK, Stop.

That's a big fat lie!

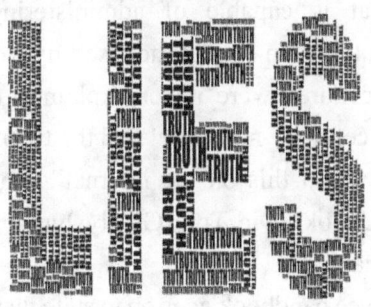

Let's Rewind and do some analysis! Phrases like *'fair and consistent'* and *'principles of natural justice'*. Did anybody at the Abbey Hotel actually know what those words meant? The answer to that is no because very few employees actually had an employee handbook.

Buzzwords like *'framework'* and *'process'* are used. OK, letme tell you how 'justice' was actually administered at the Abbey Hotel when there were issues between employees and their employer. Both parties were summoned to speak with the wages clerk.

After she left, I don't know where people went to when they had an issue.

That's it folks. Does that resemble a framework with procedures that is capable of administering justice and resolving disputes in an employment setting?

These procedures were never explained to anybody at the hotel! And certainly not to me! Did the financial controller who said he "found this on the internet" actually read this employee handbook? Did Tom Grealy Junior ever read this employment manual?

The employee handbook goes on to state that *"the essential elements of any procedure for dealing with grievance and disciplinary issues are that they be rational and fair. Good practice entails a number of stages in discipline and grievance handling. These include raising the issue with the senior management in the first instance."*

The Employee Manual further states that "the employee concerned has the right to a fair and impartial determination of the issues concerned, taking into account any representations made by, or on behalf of the employee and any other relevant or appropriate evidence, factors or circumstances." The result of this complete lack of professionalism left staff broken and demoralised.

Scripture: *"Let everything be done decently and in order."* (1 Corinthians 14 v 40)

Lesson: Make sure proper disciplinary procedures are in place to deal with grievances at work. It is worth investing in this process. It will save you, the employer much heartache in the long-run. Value your employees and they will value you.

Exercise: Out of ten, how would you rate the disciplinary/grievance procedure at your place of work?

Chapter 11
Dodgy Director's and Fraud

"Facts are a threat to those who commit fraud." (Dr DaShanne Stokes) [37]

While the thrust of this book is focussed on bullying in the workplace and the mental health consequences for employees, it is important to share this story of fraud from the Abbey Hotel because, believe it or not, the fraud has had an impact on the mental health of former managers and employees at the Abbey Hotel. The employees who were aware of the fraud feared to report this to Anya Grealy, because nobody dared speak truth about her blued eyed boys, Adrian and Tom Jnr. A former financial controller at the Abbey Hotel mysteriously left her job after she pointed out

---

[37] https://www.goodreads.com/quotes/8736192-facts-are-threatening-to-those-invested-in-fraud)

that Adrian and Tom Junior were draining the business financially. In essence, they were lazy arses and were still getting paid.

Key Witnesses

For years, a certain rumour swirled around the hotel that a certain manager was stealing money from the carvery till. One thing was certain; the carvery till was down on a regular basis.

The carvery till was operated approximately five times per week by Adrian Grealy. The carvery operated from 12:30 pm to 3 pm, approximately seven days a week. However, on the 10th October 2018, just three weeks after I left the Abbey Hotel), Frank Alesworth, who was the food and beverage manager at the Abbey Hotel, contacted me through Lily Brackstone to ask if we could meet up and discuss certain issues. We met that particular evening at 9 pm on October 10th 2018 at Casey's petrol station in Roscommon. It was clear that he was very nervous. He shared with me how Tom Grealy Junior was violating his contract of employment in relation to taking holidays. Tom Grealy Junior has a record of violating employment law in this area.

He used holiday time as a weapon to bully his staff! Tom Grealy Junior's style, when it comes to bullying and intimidation, is snake-like, subtle and covert. However, the words of philosopher *Rumi* ring true with regard to Tom Grealy Junior's behaviour, *"there are three things that cannot be hidden – the sun, the moon and the truth."*

What Frank Alesworth was to share next was a bombshell! He confided in me that he believed Adrian Grealy was stealing from the till in the carvery. This was a story that I had heard for many years in the staff canteen. Subsequent to that, a former employee confided in me that Anya Grealy hired detectives.

How true this is, I don't know. What I can confirm is that one junior employee was found to have been robbing one of the tills to the tune of three thousand euro in mid-2018. Ouch!

Two former employees of the Abbey Hotel confided in me that Tom Grealy Junior, on numerous occasions, was stealing from the restaurant till over a long period of time. These two employees would testify under oath if need be. Wouldn't the character *"Lieutenant Horatio Kane"* in the series CSI Miami love to get his hands on this case!

Looking at the company documents in February on the Company registration office website, there is a level of debt on the Abbey Hotel that is unsustainable. In February 2019, Adrian Grealy and Tom Grealy Junior and Senior were named as directors of the Abbey Hotel, while Anya Grealy was named as a secretary.[38] The *2014 Companies Act* codified much of the duties surrounding director's duties. One of the key requirements for directors is that they must exhibit a degree of due skill, care and diligence in the exercise of his/her functions. In *Re City Equitable Fire Insurance Co*[39] there are three principles set down for directors as to how they should exercise care, skill and diligence.

a) The Defendant must exercise a degree of skill that might reasonably be expected from a person of his knowledge and experience.
b) The Defendant is not bound to give continuous attention to the company but bound to attend all meetings that he/she might be expected to attend.
c) The Defendant may delegate a specific function to another person provided that the Defendant trusts the person to perform the duties honestly.

---

[38] https://www.cro.ie/Services/Company-Searchhttps://www.cro.ie/Services/Company-Search
[39] Re City Equitable Fire Insurance Co {1925} Ch. 407

Liability of directors on insolvency

One overriding statutory duty is contained in s 223 of the 2014 Companies Act, which requires that directors comply with all the requirements of the 2014 Companies Act. The result is that directors can be made personally liable for the debts of the company where certain provisions of company's legislation is not complied with, <u>especially where the conduct contributed to or lead to the insolvency of the company.</u>

S 610 of the 2104 Act dives into detail as to what powers a liquidator, examiner of company, receivers or creditors have in bringing an action against the directors in court in the event of <u>fraudulent or reckless trading</u>. Restriction of directors is governed by s 819 of the 2014 Companies Act. Honesty and responsibility are relevant criteria. The leading case is *La Moselle Clothing.* [40]

---

[40] La Moselle Clothing Ltd v Souhali {1998} 2 ILRM 551

Scripture: "But select capable men from all the people, men who fear God, trustworthy men who hate dishonest gain and appoint them as officials over thousands, hundreds, fifties and tens." (Exodus 18 v 21)

Lesson: One can conclude that Adrian and Tom Grealy Junior are not fit for the role of directors of the Abbey Hotel. The stark reality of directors being either dishonest or incompetent is that it causes tremendous hardship for the employees of a company, suppliers and creditors. It forces employees to compromise their values. As a business owner, choose wisely who you appoint as a director of your company. Let the scandal of John Delany and the Irish F.A.I. be a stark warning when appointing directors. You can copy the link below and paste it into Google and find out what a dodgy director looks like.

https://www.theguardian.com/football/2019/dec/12/fai-in-meltdown-debts-and-dysfunction-put-irish-football-in-peril

Exercise: How honest are you? If you went to an ATM machine and you saw 500 euro left behind by a previous customer, would you keep it?

Chapter 12
Health and Safety

"The use of silly and meaningless safety slogans don't matter. It creates a distraction and delusion that safety and risk are being addressed. We may feel good about speaking such words but they dumb down culture and distract people from taking safety seriously." (Dr Rob Long) [41]

---

[41] Dr Rob Long, Executive Director at Human Dimensions Pty Ltd, "All injuries are preventable and other silly sayings"
https://safetyrisk.net/all-injuries-are-preventable-and-other-silly-safety-sayings/

Whilst the thrust of this book is about exposing a culture of bullying, it is important to touch on health and safety. You may ask why? Well, you will find where bullying is rife in an employment situation, health and safety is usually in a shambles. With regard to health and safety, in the kitchen, things were going fine until late 2016, when the head chef, in consultation with the Grealy's decided that staff could no longer get their lunch from the carvery. I saw chefs take left-overs from the fridge and use it to prepare staff dinners. I saw chefs take left-over sausages from breakfast and recycle them for lunch by pouring gravy over them. In the eyes of certain chefs this was deemed acceptable! Truly disgraceful! Time for Gordon Ramsey to drop into the Abbey!

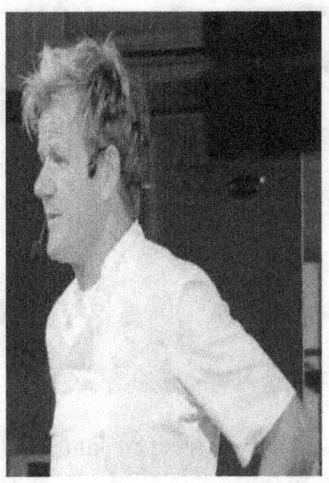

And what about the way in which mulled wine was prepared at the Abbey Hotel? Up until late 2016, mulled wine was primarily prepared fresh for each wedding. The reason I know this is because I always worked Wednesdays, Thursdays and Fridays. Most weddings took place on a Friday or Saturday. So for weddings on Friday, I would prepare the mulled wine on Friday mornings. However, I noticed that mulled wine from a wedding on a Friday wedding or indeed from a Saturday wedding would still be in the main fridge the following Wednesday when I returned to work.

The Abbey Hotel considered it acceptable to use mulled wine from the previous week for a wedding the following week. That is a fact! Head chef Eddie O' Brien oversaw and authorised this.

Then there was the incident in January 2014 when I was up in the attic with Sean *"Second Gear"* Shelton. As per normal after Christmas, all the decorations had to go back to the attic on the first floor. While I was putting away the decorations in the attic I suddenly fell through the floor of the attic and crashed through into a bathroom in a bedroom below.

I narrowly missed hitting my head off the toilet bowl as I crashed to the floor. The following day Anya Grealy asked me if I was OK. I explained to her what happened and that *"I had a lucky escape."* This was not recorded because the Abbey Hotel didn't have an incident book. If you have read this far you will know that there were little or no procedures at the Abbey Hotel.

It is actually quite shocking to think that a four-star-hotel had *no system* of recording incidences at work. Even your local crèche or school has a system to record accidents, be they children or employees who suffer an accident!

And not forgetting that Friday evening in December 2017 when the Abbey Hotel hosted a Christmas party for various different companies in the region. Adrian Grealy was on that night. Unfortunately, Adrian was on duty under the influence of alcohol.

Worse still, his mother, Anya, was on duty and DID NOT SEND HIM HOME. This was a blatant breach of duty of care to the staff and to the GUESTS. It is at this stage that you realise that Anya Grealy is DELUSIONAL. These events were witnessed by restaurant staff/management as well as the porters.

Scripture: *"But the Lord is faithful, and he will strengthen you and protect you from the evil one."* (2 Thessalonians 3 v 3))

Lesson: Employers, I have some advice. Making sure that your employees are safe doesn't have to cost a fortune. Genuinely caring about employee safety and a dash of common sense will go a long way ensure health and safety is cost effective in the workplace.

Exercise: How would you rate your application of health and safety legislation out of ten?

Chapter 13
Invasion of Privacy

1. Introduction

You are probably wondering what surveillance has to do with bullying. I assure you, the two are very much connected. Let's take the example of dictatorships! What do dictators do to control their subjects? They spy on them. Big brother is not a new phenomenon. It simply has taken on a new and sinister format because of the range of sophisticated technology available in the year 2022. You see, people like Tom Grealy Junior are assholes in the eyes of the employees at the Abbey Hotel.

However, real leaders command respect from their team because real leaders SERVE. Tom Grealy Junior on the other hand, dictates. In order to punch home my message, let me share with you a story of HOW LITTLE RESPECT this chap has for his parents. In May 2018, when there was an issue regarding the set up for weddings in the ballroom,

I told him the only people I answered to were his parents, Tom and Anya. His response shocked me to the core! He replied *"I don't want to fucking hear about Tom and Anya Grealy."*

1. <u>Now to the business of analysing the legislation on CCTV</u>

There is a tough balancing act between respecting employee's privacy and the employer's right to maintain and protect his business. Any person or organisation that collects and processes the personal data of individuals is considered a *'data controller'*.

For this reason, any usage of a CCTV system must be considered in light of the obligations imposed by data legislation on data controllers, and implemented in accordance with the principles of data protection. So what are the legal requirements in this jurisdiction with regard to the use of CCTV?

A) Your employer must inform you if there is CCTV in your workplace

The employer needs to display signs telling you where the cameras are located. Jack Danson and Carl Carpenter informed me that this did not happen at the Abbey Hotel until they pointed it out at a disciplinary hearing. The signs should be easy to read, well-lit and positioned in places where they can be easily seen. The signs should also provide contact details for someone whom you can discuss the processing of your data with, for example the owner of the premises or the security company operating the CCTV system. [42]

---

[42] Data protection Act 2018 and ARTICLE 4 (7) EU General Data Protection Regulation

B) <u>Your employer must clearly state why they are using CCTV if it is not obvious</u>

For example, the reason for having the camera placed at the entrance of a building to detect intruders would be obvious. If your employer is using CCTV to monitor your behaviour or performance, this is not obvious and the employer must inform before recording for those reasons. [43]

Similarly, if CCTV is installed for health and safety reasons, this should be clearly stated and made known to everybody in the workplace.

C) <u>Your employer should have a written CCTV policy which includes the following</u>:

- "The identity of the company holding the CCTV footage
- The reasons why the CCTV footage is being used

---

[43] Article 5(1) (b) EU General Data Protection Regulations

- Any third parties the footage may be given to
- How long the footage can be held for
- How the footage will be secured."[44]

D) <u>Reasonable and unreasonable use of CCTV</u>

CCTV to constantly monitor employees would be intrusive and would only be justified in special circumstances. Monitoring you (the employee), without you knowing, is generally against the law. It is against the law to collect someone's data or monitor them without them knowing. This is known as covert surveillance. This is only used in <u>special circumstances</u> where the data will be used to detect, prevent or investigate crime or to apprehend and prosecute offenders. You should only be monitored covertly if you or your workplace is relevant to a criminal investigation. Covert surveillance must be focussed and only last for a short time.

---

[44] See Articles 5, 12, 13, and 14 EU GDPR in particular regarding transparency obligations

If no evidence is found within a reasonable amount of time, the employer should stop the covert surveillance. [45]

E) A specific written policy must be put in place to allow for covert surveillance

This policy must detail the purpose and justification for the covert surveillance and provide details of the procedures, measures and safeguards that will be implemented while this type of surveillance is on-going.

The objective of the covert surveillance should be the involvement of An Garda Siochana or other prosecution authorities who can investigate any alleged criminal offences(s). This should be added to the policy. [46]

Data that is kept for longer than one month in the case of CCTV would be hard to justify. Access to the data should be

---

[45] http://fitzsimonsredmond.ie/the-use-of-cctv-in-the-workplace/ and Deegan v Dunne Stores {2014} 2 JIEC 206 (Employment Appeals Tribunal)

[46] Article 5(1) (b) General Data Protection Regulations

restricted to authorised personnel and it should be stored in a safe place. [47]

2. I Spy with my little eye

About two years before I left the Abbey Hotel, at least 25 extra cameras were installed around the hotel. Was this a reaction to the 'apparent disappearance' of 10,000 euro and a fair amount of beer barrels? Perhaps the Abbey Hotel is haunted!

One of the areas that the Abbey Hotel installed a camera was in the staff canteen. I don't know about you but would you like somebody looking over your shoulder when you are having your lunch. If you can't trust your staff while eating lunch then clearly you don't TRUST YOUR STAFF AT ALL. I suggest that employers sit down with the employees and deal with the issues that have brought both employer and employee to this level of distrust.

3. <u>The Magnificent Tea Drinking Seven</u>

---

[47] https://employmentrightsireland.com/tag/cctv/

After I left the Abbey Hotel, I was informed by a current member of staff that seven staff members were issued written warnings BEFORE they were issued verbal warnings. At that stage, there was just a small paragraph on the Abbey Hotel's famous 103-page Human Resource Manual about CCTV.

At the time of writing this, Matilda Leavenworth, who is dealing with human resource issues at the Abbey Hotel, was NOT a qualified human resource manager. This is no time for having unqualified staff in the area of human resource management.

More recently, seven members of staff were reprimanded for apparently taking longer than they should at their break. Whether they were innocent or guilty I don't know. In terms of how the Abbey Hotel has used CCTV surveillance in the past, it is a well-known FACT that Tom Grealy Senior, SPIED on staff from his own computer in his house which is ADJACENT to the Abbey Hotel. Staff could cite countless examples of Tom Grealy Senior ringing various staff members telling them they needed to change the channel on the television in the bar.

He made no secret of it that he was WATCHING them via CCTV! I have heard stories about Adrian Grealy and

Frank Alesworth having apps on their phone which were connected to the mainframe CCTV unit at the Abbey Hotel; to spy on staff. How true this is I don't know!

4. Case Study

It is worth looking at a recent High Court case [48] where a hospice employee won a High Court appeal over the use of data from CCTV footage in a disciplinary investigation into unauthorised breaks and staff room graffiti saying *"Kill all whites, ISIS is my life."* After you have read the details of the High Court case, apply it to the situation at the Abbey Hotel and come to your own conclusions.

Cormac Doolin had appealed a Circuit Court decision that his data rights were not breached as a result of the use of information from CCTV footage for a disciplinary investigation into the graffiti. The other issue appealed was that of the taking of unauthorised breaks in the hospice staff room. Ms Justice Niamh Hyland allowed his appeal saying there was no evidence for the Circuit Court conclusion that the CCTV footage, or material derived from it for the disciplinary hearing, was for security purposes.

She also found the data protection commissioner, against whom Mr. Doolin brought the original appeal over the use of

---

[48] Cormac Doolin V The Data Protection Commissioner and Our Lady's Hospice and Care Service, {2020} IEHC 90

the information, made an error of law in holding that no further processing of the CCTV data took place. The Commissioner's conclusion was founded on an incorrect interpretation of 'processing' under the terms of the Data Protection Act 1988, she said. [49]

The judge did not accept the commissioner's claim that such a *"finding would be draconian and seriously hamper investigations of this type."* Judge Hyland noted that a sign beside the CCTV camera at the time of the graffiti incident in November 2015 said, *"images are recorded for the purposes of health and safety and crime prevention."* By August 2016, the hospice had amended this policy to state the system was to *"prevent crime and promote staff security and public safety."* It added: "If, in the event of viewing CCTV for the specified purpose, a disciplinary action is observed, the CCTV can be used for the purpose of a disciplinary investigation." [50] The facts of this case can be differentiated with that of the Abbey Hotel, Roscommon in that there was no staff security or criminal issues. It was simply a case of *"had the boys been drinking tea longer than they should have?"*

Ms Justice Hyland said if at the time of the graffiti incident that new policy was in operation "none of the above difficulties would have arisen." Where purposes for the use of CCTV are clearly identified, and assuming all other permissible purposes under the law, then the use of such material is likely to be uncontroversial, she said. She was

---

[49] https://beta.courts.ie/acc/alfresco/d08c47b8-1bf6-4101-b072-dd45536fa56b/2020_IEHC_90.pdf/pdf
[50] ibid 49

therefore overturning the Circuit Court's decision as there was no evidence for the conclusion that the disciplinary action against Mr Cummins, in which information from the CCTV footage was used, was carried out for security purposes.

Mr. Doolin became subject of a disciplinary investigation in November 2015 into *"an offensive graffiti message"* carved into a table in the staff room and the use of unauthorised breaks.

At an investigation meeting on December 1, Mr. Doolin said "if work got on top of us, we would take a break," and go to the staff room. He accepted he should have said he was taking a break to his manager. He refused to watch the CCTV at that time and later made a complaint to the data protection commissioner that data retrieved from the CCTV was used in an incorrect/unfair manner that led to an illegal sanction against him.

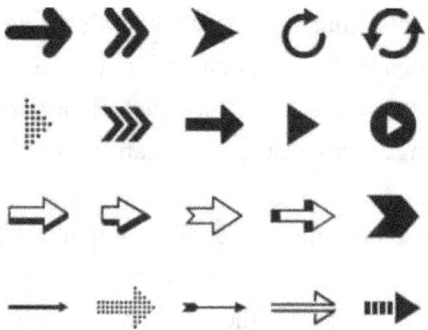

The hospices argued that there was a legitimate justification to access and view the footage. The commissioner found that while the information gathered from viewing the footage may have been used for a purpose other than the initial one of investigating a security incident, the use of them in disciplinary proceedings did "not constitute a different purpose." [51]

Mr Justice Hyland said there was a 'surprising shift' by the Commissioner during the life of the proceedings from asserting initially there was no further processing of the footage "to asserting in these proceedings (there was) no breach because any further processing was done for the purpose for which the material was collected", i.e. security. The idea that the information from the CCTV in the context of disciplinary proceedings was for security purposes rather than disciplinary "does not find a basis in any of the material

---

[51] ibid 49 and https://www.irishtimes.com/news/crime-and-law/courts/high-court/use-of-cctv-footage-in-disciplinary-process-breached-data-rights-1.4180806

before me. There is simply no evidence at all to this effect," she said. [52]

The judge adjourned the matter to allow the parties to consider her judgment and to argue whether it should be sent back to the Commissioner for further consideration.

One other notable case of abuse of CCTV is the Spanish case of *Lopez Ribalda & Ors v Spain*. [53] This case was decided in the European Court of Justice in favour of the employee.

---

[52] ibid 49 and http://fitzsimonsredmond.ie/the-use-of-cctv-in-the-workplace/

[53] Lopez Ribalda and ORS v Spain {2019} ECHR 752

Part 3
Let's Go Deep

Chapter 14
Brothers at War

1. Introduction

From the earliest times, history has recorded stories of sibling rivalries like Cain and Abel to Jacob and Esau in the scriptures. These ancient accounts of power struggles illustrate the wickedness of men's hearts and that a man is prepared to steal and kill his brother out of sheer jealousy. [54]

The Abbey Hotel had its own sibling rivalry in the guise of Adrian and Tom Grealy Junior. They were like two-year-olds throwing a tantrum when things didn't go their way.

---

[54] Genesis 4 v 6-8, Genesis 27 v 47 and Genesis 37 v 18

During my tumultuous six years at the Abbey Hotel, the competition between these two brothers was fierce. It caused tremendous hardship for the staff that had to deal with these two bickering buffoons. Jealousy is a deadly disease. Beware, lest it take hold of any of you. It will consume you until it eventually destroys you and those around you.

2. Sibling Rivalry

Sibling rivalry is defined as *"an intense competition among siblings for recognition and the attention of their parents."* [55] Sibling rivalry usually begins when a baby is introduced to a family and the older child fears that he/she will be replaced by the new-born baby. An older child can become extremely jealous and become aggressive toward the baby. [56]The rivalry between siblings actively involved in a family-owned business takes two different forms: emotional and strategic.

To find solutions to resolve conflicts among brothers and sisters in family businesses, one must determine if the rivalry

---

[55] https://www.britannica.com/science/sibling-rivalry
[56] ibid 55

is emotional or strategic, or some combination of both. One must recognise that that the primary problem is not, in fact, between the siblings but rather between each child and the need for recognition from his or her parent. [57]Consequently, the solution is not working with the sibling relationship, but with the relationship between the adult and the parent.

The second type of sibling rivalry is rooted in conflict over business styles and strategies, rather than family emotions. Frequently, such strategic conflict is driven by differences in personality concerning levels of financial risk. The sibling conflict in the Holstrom family illustrates a strategy-based case of rivalry.

An opportunity to diversify the business through an acquisition became available to John and Jim who were co-owners of the business they inherited from their father. [58]

---

[57] Dean Fowler and Peg Masterson Edquist, *"Rivalry can Destroy Family Business"* Milwaukee Business Journal (February 29th, 2004)

[58] ibid 57

This is a most familiar and time-tested story. A family business is started, for years run by the founder who knows every detail in every crevasse that exists to make it work. Enter the children who, after having spent many summers through their adolescent and college years working there, are tested and scrutinised in every way to determine their acumen in the business world. The moment of truth is upon them as they prepare to take their place in the business: who is the best suited to take over? [59]

Tom Grealy Junior was given the hotel to run on his 40th birthday. It soon became clear that hotel was suffering after he took over. People who would normally dine at the hotel stopped coming. They were used to a warm and cheery smile from Anya. Now they were met with the surly and miserable face of Tom Grealy Junior at the door. Anya Grealy promptly took back control of the hotel and the downward spiral in the hotel's fortunes receded. It was clear to Anya that her son was not ready to take command of the hotel. Giving things to children or indeed adults before they are ready is always a recipe for disaster. It became clear to me and other key staff that Tom Grealy Junior was prepared to do just about anything to ensure his brother, Adrian, was no longer in the running for the position of General Manager of the hotel.

When brothers can't agree in business as was the case in *Murph's Restaurant*, the end result is disastrous. [60]The court ordered the business to be wound up.

---

[59] ibid 57
[60] Re Murphs Restaurant Ltd {1979} ILRM 141

This case is a warning to warring siblings. A court will wind up a business where sibling rivalry has become so bad that the only solution is to actually wind up the business. Now it's time for some spiritual refreshment.

Scripture: *"He who says He loves God but hates his brother is not in the light."* (1 John 4 v 20)

Lesson: Angela Civitella from her own personal experience shares her wisdom:

1. "Respect and honour your sibling.
2. Develop your own brand of friendship.
3. Recognise each other's strengths while encouraging your differences.
4. Celebrate each other's successes". [61]

---

[61] https://www.forbes.com/sites/forbescoachescouncil/2017/10/16/how-siblings-can-overcome-rivalry-in-a-family-business/

Exercise: Another question! Out of ten, how well do you get on with your siblings? This question is only applicable if you are in business with a sibling or a family member.

Chapter 15
Rooting Out Toxicity

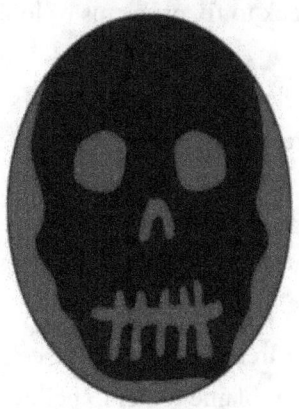

1. Introduction

It is my observation that toxic people in the workplace generally are looking out for themselves. Leaders look out for their teams, even before they are in a formal leadership position. Toxic leaders often have two different faces, one they show to management, and one they show to their own team. They rule by fear. What they lack is empathy and concern for people and that ultimately won't take them closer to their goals. So it's easy to see through them because it's just a ploy to get ahead. [62]

2. The Toxicity Test

So how do you find out if YOU are toxic? Let's look at some questions!

- What is more valuable to you? Being your employer's henchman or the respect of your co-workers?
- Do you seek to fix problems or look for somebody to blame?
- Do you celebrate your co-workers success or do you always brag on your own success?
- Do you use fear as a motivator?
- Do you take the time to know the person that work for you or is it all about you?

Can you see a trend here? If you seek praise from your employer, seek to blame others, believe fear is a good motivator and don't know your employees, well guess what, You ARE TOXIC. Call Alex Polizzi and let her guide you if you are in the hotel industry!

---

[62] https://louisjfernandez.com/2019/07/08/id-toxic-leaders-before-its-too-late/

3. Indicators of toxicity

You are looking for someone that places the organisation above their colleagues and that accepts praise without reciprocating. If you ask them what they think of their peers and they have mostly negative things to say, then you most likely have a toxic leader. When something goes wrong, see if they tell you who was at fault or if they focus instead on how to fix the problem.

Teams with a high staff turnover rate and a bad health and safety record will usually have toxic leaders. Toxic employees lack creativity and do the bare minimum and leave the first chance they get. Let's face it; most people don't like their boss. [63]

Millions of people are bullied at work every year. It is literally KILLING your business. You are rotting from the head down. It's time to wake up and smell the coffee!

Scripture: "Bad company destroys good character." (1 Corinthians 15 v 33)

---

[63] Ibid 62

Lesson: Don't let toxic people destroy you. Either root them out of your life or move on and build a circle of friends that build you up and encourage you.

Exercise: Out of ten, how toxic is your workplace?

Part 4
Time for Change

change.org

What would you change?

Chapter 16
Make My Day Punk

"All plots tend to move deathward. This is the nature of plots. Political plots, terrorist plots, lovers' plots, narrativeplots, plots that are part of children's games.

We edge nearer death every time we plot. It is like a contract that all must sign, the plotters as well as those who are the targets of the plot." [64] *(Don DeLillo)*

---

[64] Don DeLillo, "White noise", (Penguin Publishing, 1985)

On Thursday, August 23rd, 2018, I was scheduled to work at 8 am. Jack Danson, on the previous evening, asked if "I could make it in by 7.30 am" as there was a bus tour that needed a hand with luggage the next morning.

He further stated that if I couldn't make it in at 7.30 am, it wasn't a big deal. I answered him that "I should be able to make it in." As it turned out, I made it in by 7.50 am. That morning, I rang the night porter Chuck Bramley at 7.10 am and asked him if he could bring down a few bags for me, just to ensure the bus would leave on time. As it turned out, Chuck Bramley never did bring down any bags. No surprise there!

All bags were on the bus at 8.32 am. The bus was originally scheduled to leave at 8.30 am for Strokestown, but due to circumstances regarding their destination (Strokestown), they would not be departing till 8.45 am. Bottom line, the bus left on time. Adrian Grealy got bitchy with me about not being in at 7 am. I knew this was going to be a tough day.

Memories of that verbal in the ballroom years ago with Adrian came flooding back. I had a sense there was going to be more trouble by the end of the day.

Later that morning, I was informed by Ciara on wash-up that I was no longer responsible for checking in the alcohol/spirits order on Thursday. I was now relieved of that duty. Ciara would now do this job. <u>*In six years at the*</u> Abbey Hotel, my judgment or integrity had never been questioned in this sphere of work. The person responsible for this decision was either Frank Alesworth or Tom Grealy Junior.

If the management had an issue with my performance it should have been POINTED out to me! But the snake that is Tom Grealy Junior is now getting exposed for the fraud that he really is.

Plotting Evil

Here is the final scene before I walked out of that God forsaken shithole of a hotel that parades itself as a four-star-hotel but in reality, is a den of iniquity. On Thursday 23rd August, the incident that sparked me to walk out of the Abbey Hotel is as follows. I was clearing bottle skips. Tom Grealy passed me on the way to his car.

He commented in a snide tone, "Iron your shirt and tuck it in." When Tom Grealy Junior made this remark, he was on the move towards his car and was approximately 3-4 yards away from me. My back was turned to Tom Grealy Junior, as I was outside clearing the bottle banks. It would be very hard for him to ascertain if my shirt was ironed, being that distance away from me; with my back turned and the fact that I was wearing a waistcoat.

His tone was arrogant and full of sarcasm. I answered Tom Grealy NOT A WORD. He hopped into his BMW and drove away. I then proceeded towards the clock-in machine which is located inside the back door of the hotel, approximately eight yards away from where I was working; clocked out and drove home. I rang Jack Danson and informed him of what had just transpired. I then did a Facebook live and shared my story. The full video is on Facebook. Click on the link below to view that earth shattering Facebook live that let my home town know how sick and twisted the Grealy family really are.

https://www.facebook.com/cathal.finnegan.14/videos/1933364536720991/UzpfSTEwMDAwMTQyMzkwNTAzNDoxOTQ0MzY5NjkyMjg3MTQy/?eid=ARD4ERzb0Dov1iFg5GbX15D44wSdsEjisIMPDXWNiOysFBmkKfM0E_J-S54Y-5Cwnem8QiTZTL4gxj

Kristin Kirkland, wife of Jack Kirkland and a former employee of the Abbey Hotel, rang me straight after the Facebook live to thank me for exposing the culture of bullying that existed in the Abbey Hotel. Tom Grealy, like his brother, Adrian, and their father, Tom Senior, had a habit of setting people up to fall. Their plan to get rid of me has backfired. This book offers irrefutable evidence of the corrupt dynasty that is the Abbey Hotel.

Scripture: *"When the kings of the earth who committed adultery with her and shared her luxury see the smoke of her burning they will weep and mourn over her."* (Revelation 18 v 9)

Lesson: "Greed is not a successful business model." (Jack Ma)

Exercise: Out of ten, how likely are you to walk away from your job.

Chapter 17
The Day of Battle

So nine weeks after leaving the Abbey Hotel on August 23rd 2018, I filed a lawsuit against the Abbey Hotel with the Workplace Relations Commission. I must confess, it was difficult writing up my submission to the WRC. The first hearing in April 2019 was postponed till August 29th due to an administrative error plus a late submission by the Abbey Hotel. That first WRC hearing was a tense affair. The Abbey Hotel, predictable as ever, used intimidation tactics by having their barrister, their solicitor, the new human resources manager, along with Anya Grealy and Tom Grealy Junior. My lawyer felt I should attend on my own first and had advised me to let the WRC hearing run its course. The hearing lasted two and a half hours. It was tough but it also gave me great experience in mooting. The adjudicator felt that the matter needed a further hearing and so, on October 22nd, I went toe to toe with the Abbey Hotel again.

What the Abbey Hotel didn't know was that a former member of the Abbey Hotel was going to testify on my behalf at the second WRC hearing. That former employee was Layla Wandsworth. She shared her story and how Tom Grealy violated employment law. Layla shared what happened during the last eight months of her tenure at the Abbey Hotel. In March 2017, Layla booked fourteen days holidays during the month of October. However, a few days before Layla was to go on holiday, Tom Grealy Junior asked Layla to return two days earlier from her holidays. Layla did so but reluctantly. It cost her 110 euro to change her flight. The Abbey Hotel never refunded her the cost of having to change her flight. On Wednesday, 11th of March 2020, I received a letter from the WRC that I was unsuccessful in my claim against the Abbey Hotel. Was I disappointed? Yes.

Was I surprised? No. The decision is now being appealed to the Labour Court in Dublin. It is clear that this organisation needs to be either scrapped or radically overhauled.

Scripture: *"But thanks be to God who always gives us the victory through Christ Jesus."* (1 Corinthians 15 v 57)

Lesson: If at first you don't succeed, then try again.

Exercise: When you face setbacks, how likely are you to persevere and try again? Mark yourself out of ten.

Chapter 18
Appeal to the Labour Court

Introduction

1. The test for constructive dismissal

There are two tests in relation to proving that a Constructive Dismissal has occurred. These are the *'Contract Test' and the 'Reasonableness Test'*.

(A) The Contract Test

In Western Excavating (ECC) Ltd v Sharp [1978] IRLR 27 the *'contract test'* is summarised as follows:

"If the employer is guilty of conduct which is a significant breach going to the root of the contract of employment, or which shows that the employer no longer intends to be bound by one or more of the essential terms of the contract, then the employee is entitled to treat himself as discharged from any other performance." (As per Lord Denning)

So what were practical examples of breaches that went to the root of my contract?

Well, in order for me to do my job I must be ALLOWED to do my job in peace and without being harassed or bullied. It came to the point where mentally and emotionally, I was drained after six years of trying to do my job. I had simply come to the realisation that my employer had breached his statutory duty of care. I was STOPPED and deliberately IMPEDED by all four of the Grealy family members from performing my duties. The two biggest culprits were Adrian and Tom Grealy Junior. There came a point where I could no longer turn a blind eye to health and safety issues at the Abbey Hotel. I had a legal and moral duty to blow the whistle on the breach of both employment and company law by all four members of the Grealy family.

I was offered a job by the Abbey Hotel and I accepted their offer in 2012. There was intent to create legal relations and the consideration was an agreed weekly wage. If you hire someone to do a job, you don't then verbally abuse them and indeed all of the conditions that are wrapped up in the contract that are vital to fulfil the contract. I had no option but to discharge myself from the contract because the breaches were fundamental breaches and went to the root of the contract.

(A) The Reasonableness Test

In addressing the reasonable test' the decision summarises the conduct of the employer as follows: "whether the employer conducts himself or his affairs so unreasonably that the employee cannot fairly be expected to put up with it any longer, if so, the employee is justified in leaving."

The requirement to substantially utilise internal procedures is an essential element of succeeding in a claim of constructive dismissal.

This is set out in the case of *Conway v Ulster Bank Ltd (UD 474/1981)* whereby the EAT said that:

"The appellant did not act reasonably in resigning without first having substantially utilised the grievance procedure to attempt to remedy her complaints."

In relation to availing of a grievance procedure, the Labour Court held as follows in *Mr O v An Employer (no. 2)* [2005] 16 E.L.R. 132:

"The court accepts that in normal circumstances a complainant who seeks to invoke the reasonableness test in furtherance of such a claim must also act reasonably by providing the employer with an opportunity to address whatever grievance they may have.

However, there is authority for the proposition that this is not a fixed or universally applicable rule and there can be situations in which a failure to give prior formal notice of grievance will not be fatal."

See Allen v Independent Newspapers [2002] E.L.R. 84;
May v Moog Ltd [2002] E.L.R. 261
Monaghan v Sherry Bros [2003] E.L.R. 293.
See also New Era Packaging v A Worker [2001] E.L.R. 122)

2. Points being appealed to the Labour Court

(A) Section 1 (b) of the Unfair Dismissals Acts 1977–2007 defines constructive dismissal as:

"the termination by the employee of his contract of employment with his employer, whether prior notice of the termination was or was not given to the employer, in circumstances in which, because of the conduct of the employer, the employee was or would have been entitled, or it was or would have been reasonable for the employee to terminate the contract of employment without giving prior notice of the termination to the employer."

(B) The other small issue that I want to deal with is that of my contract not being renewed upon re-joining the Abbey Hotel in September 2015. I had officially ended my employment with them in April 2014 although the p45 didn't arrive until another month later. My conditions of employment were different in terms of hours, days and responsibilities.

The Abbey Hotel failed in their responsibility to give me a new contract. Relevant legislation is The Terms of employment (Information Acts 1994-2004) *(See also A Solicitor v A Solicitors Firm*

(C) I did not get adequate breaks (S 12, Organisation of Working Time Act 1977)

NOTE: The summary judgment (10 pages) of my case can be accessed on the WRC website (www.workplacerelations.ie). The citation is Porter v Hotel and the Adjudication number is ADJ-00017919

With regard to my appeal to the Labour court a lot has changed since I the case was hear at the WRC. The case was due to heard on the 31/3/21. This information was relayed to me by the Labour Court approximately five weeks before the date of the hearing. Immediately I informed the Labour court that I wanted to subpoena witnesses. They me that I needed to speak with legal counsel from the Abbey Hotel. It took me three weeks to get hold of the law firm representing the Abbey Hotel. To make a long story short the Labour court decided they would not allow me to subpoena witnesses. Please see on the next page the response from the Labour Court as to why they would not allow me to subpoena witnesses.

Sent: 22 March 2021 13:29

To: cathalhonkey@outlook.com

Subject: UD/20/100, CD/20/141, TE/20/36 Abbey Hotel Ltd (Liam J. Sheridan & Co.) - and - Cathal Finnegan

Re: UD/20/100, CD/20/141, TE/20/36 Abbey Hotel Ltd (Liam J. Sheridan & Co.) - and - Cathal Finnegan

"Dear Mr Finnegan,

The Chairman has decided to refuse your request for postponement of a scheduled hearing. The Court is not in receipt of any valid request for issuance of a subpoena to any individual. Any such request would require, at a minimum, to provide current address details of any intended recipient and to have been made in good time before the date of hearing. In this case the Court was previously provided with a list of names in the context of a request for postponement of a hearing but no request was made to draw up subpoenas.

Any request for the issuance by the Court of a subpoena would require, as mentioned above, details of address of the intended witness and clarification as to the reason the subpoena is sought. Specifically, any request for subpoena must include information as to whether the party requesting a subpoena has requested the intended witness to give evidence and confirmation that the intended witness has refused to do so. In addition, the applicant must share with the Court a summary outline of the relevant evidence to be adduced from the witness as regards matters of fact which are in dispute and of which the intended witness has direct knowledge.

This Hearing will go ahead as scheduled on 31/3/21 at 10.30 am.

Yours sincerely,
Andrew Gavin

The Labour Court"

Conclusion: When we are sick we go to a qualified doctor. It should be the same for those adjudicating on employment matters. If the WRC is to be reformed then <u>barristers (Senior Counsel) should be adjudicating</u>. With regard to the decision of the Labour Court not allowing me to subpoena witnesses, it is clear that they are not interested in administering justice. It's interesting to note that the hearing would be via video link which violates Constitutional requirements for justice to be administered in public according to Article 34 of the Irish Constitution. I made the decision that it was pointless getting the decision of the Labour court judicially reviewed. What is required is a root and branch reform of both the W.R.C and Labour court.

The Labour Court is just another tick box exercise for the Irish Legal System. Irelands former Director General of the Irish Law Society, Ken Murphy stated earlier this year in an interview with the Irish Independent that advancing technology will mean that it is only a matter of time before judges are replaced by artificial intelligence. Computers with sophisticated algorithms will <u>replace judges</u>. The full article can be accessed on www.independent.ie. The element of bias and unfairness will be removed from the decision making process. It will root out bias, bad decisions and corruption.

Scripture: "One day Jesus told his disciples a story to show them they that they should always pray and never give up." (Luke 18 v 1)

Lesson: It's not over till you win.

Exercise: After having read the book thus far, how confident would you be in bringing an employment issue before the WRC? Answer the question out of a likelihood from 1-10.

Chapter 19
Setback

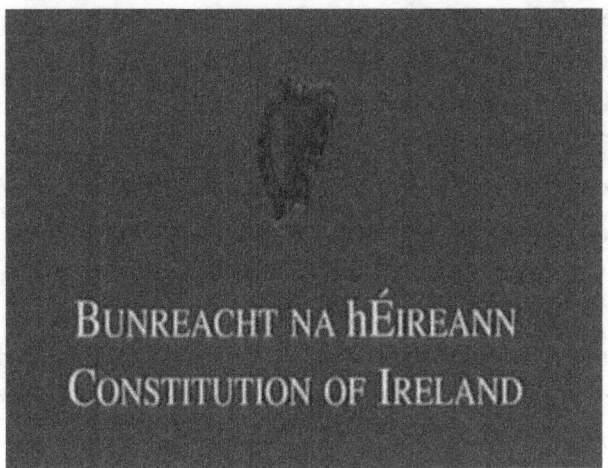

Article 30.3.1 of the Constitution of Ireland provides

"The State guarantees in its laws to respect, and, as far as practicable, by its laws to defend and vindicate the personal rights of the citizen."

Introduction

The High Court has rejected a challenge to the constitutionality of the Workplace Relations Commission ('WRC'). Judgement in the case of *Zalewski v Workplace Relations Commission IEHC 178 {2020}* was given on 21st April 2020. Mr Zalewski argued that the WRC was unconstitutional for two reasons. Firstly, he argued that the WRC carries out the administration of justice in breach of the constitutional rule that (with limited exceptions) only the courts may administer justice. Secondly, he argued that several of the statutory procedures of the WRC were so deficient that they failed to vindicate his personal rights. The High Court rejected both arguments.

The WRC does not exercise judicial functions. On the issue of the exercise of judicial functions, the High Court held that, while the WRC shares many of the attributes of a court, the WRC does not carry out the administration of justice. A crucial function that is not conferred on the WRC is the ability to enforce its own decisions. A court can enforce its orders, whereas a party seeking to enforce a WRC decision must seek enforcement through the district court. When a party seeks to enforce an order of the WRC re-instatement or reengagement under the Unfair Dismissals Acts, the District Court has the power to modify the form of redress by ordering compensation instead of re-instatement or reengagement. The High court found that this provision allows the District court to overrule the decision made by the WRC. The High court considered this to be "a significant curtailment of the decision-making powers," of the WRC. [65]

Accordingly, the High Court determined that:

"A decision-maker who is not only reliant on the parties invoking the judicial power to enforce its decisions, but whose decisions as part of that process, cannot be said to be carrying out the administration." So the statutory procedures of the WRC are not unconstitutional.

Mr Zalewski set out four alleged procedural deficiencies in the statutory procedures of the WRC. He argued that these alleged deficiencies have the effect of infringing his constitutional rights. The High Court considered each of the alleged deficiencies.

1. In order to be appointed, adjudication officers of the WRC are not required to have any legal qualification or experience. The High Court decided that it was necessary for officers of a body such as the WRC that is not carrying out a judicial function) to have the type of legal qualifications that would be required of people being appointed to carry out a judicial function. Based on evidence presented, the High Court was not satisfied that the absence of a statutory requirement resulted in any systematic failure in the hearing and adjudication of claims at the WRC.
2. The fact that evidence at the WRC is not taken on oath was not accepted by the High Court to

---

[65] https://byrnewallace.com/news-and-recent-work/publications/high-court-upholds-the-constitutionality-of-the-workplace

necessarily be a procedural deficiency. The court determined that there was "much to be said for informality of hearings before the WRC that conferred great advantages to claimants in terms of the speed of hearings".
3. Mr. Zalewski argued that the absence of a statutory right of cross-examination is a major flaw in the statutory procedures of the WRC.

The High court found that adjudication officers of the WRC have an implied power to allow cross-examination. Not every case gives rise to a right of a party to cross-examine witnesses; this will depend on the circumstances of each case. In cases where cross-examination is required and the adjudication officer fails to allow cross-examination, this would represent a good ground for judicial review in the particular circumstances of the case. However, the absence of an express right to cross-examine in all cases is not unconstitutional.

4. The High Court rejected the argument that the fact that the hearings of the WRC are not in public is a procedural deficiency. [66]

Article 34.1 of the Constitution of Ireland provides:

"Justice shall be administered in courts established by law by judges appointed in the manner provided by this

---

[66] https://www.beauchamps.ie/publications/881

Constitution, and, save in such special and limited cases as may be prescribed by law, shall be administered in public."

The constitutional requirement that justice should be administered in public does not need to be 'read across' to decision-making by non-judicial bodies. There is nothing inherently objectionable in prescribing a procedure which allows an administrative decision-making to make certain types of determinations on the basis of an informal hearing conducted in private.

Prior to the decision of 21st April 2020, other aspects of this case had already been decided in the High Court and successfully appealed to the Supreme Court. This decision was appealed and below are the key takeaways from the decision.

The landmark Supreme Court decision of *Zalewski v Adjudication Officer and WRC, Ireland and the Attorney General* [2021] IESC 24 has brought about key procedural changes in terms of how employment disputes are determined in the Workplace Relations Commission ("WRC").

The Supreme Court held that although the WRC was engaged in the administration of justice, Article 37 of the Constitution expressly granted a power to non-judicial bodies to exercise 'limited functions and powers of a judicial nature'.

However, the Supreme Court, whilst criticising the lack of an express provision to allow cross-examination in the WRC, held that the following two procedural aspects of the WRC were incompatible and repugnant to the Constitution:

1. The blanket prohibition on WRC hearings being held in public pursuant to s. 41(13) of the Workplace

Relations Act 2015 and s. 8(6) of the Unfair Dismissals Act 1977, as amended; and
2. The absence of any provision for the administration of an oath or the cross-examination of witnesses in the WRC under Part 4 of the Workplace Relations Act 2015 or s. 8 of the Unfair Dismissals Act 1977.

Effect of Zalewski on Future WRC Hearings

The Supreme Court's ruling in Zalewski has brought about a number of welcomed and indeed long overdue changes to the operation of the WRC, effective from 6 April 2021:

- All WRC hearings involving the administration of justice are open to the public now and parties' names will not be anonymised. This change can act as an additional negotiation tool for employees, as adverse publicity can have serious reputational repercussions for employers involved in a WRC hearing.
- Where there is a direct conflict of evidence before the WRC, the Adjudicating Officer is empowered to administer an oath or affirmation. Whilst requiring a witness to swear an oath does not dramatically increase hearing costs, the introduction of written witness statements like in the UK could increase costs substantially and add to hearing time.
- New cross-examination guidelines for witnesses and a penalty for giving false evidence will be introduced. Legislation from the Oireachtas (legislature) is expected on this shortly.

Conclusion

Whilst the Zalewski decision is welcome from a fair-procedures point of view, it remains to be seen whether the decision will result in a more robust delivery of justice for all invloved. It is my personal opinion that barristers (Senior Counsel) should be adjudicating on decisions at the WRC as opposed to lay people.

Scripture: *"Let everything be done decently and in order."* (1 Corinthians 14 v 40)

Lesson: Our country needs to return to the values that are enshrined in our Constitution.

Exercise: Out of a score of 1-10 do you think the High Court made the right decision?

Part 5
Breaking the Cycle

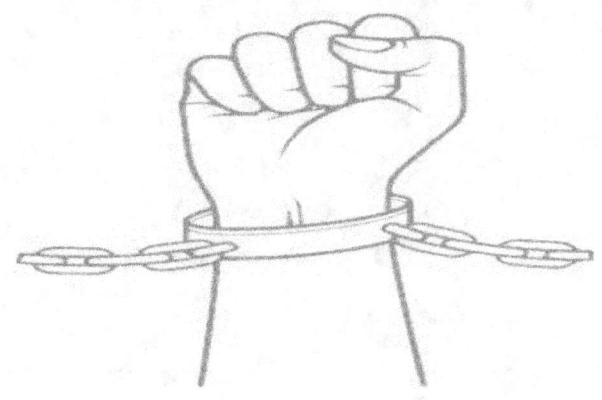

Chapter 20
Beating the Fear Factor

An Employee's Checklist to counter bullying

1. Value yourself.
2. Never let anybody walk over you.
3. If you have been bullied and never dealt with it then go deal with otherwise it will follow you until you look that devil in the eye and say "Enough is enough."
4. Stay away from toxic people at work.
5. Hang out with 'the good folk' at your place of work.

6. Choose your job carefully, research your potential employer.
7. Read up on employment law and stay abreast of developments.

8. Read that employment contract before you sign it.
9. In particular, read the disciplinary/grievance procedures. Check to see if they are in line with current legislation. You would be surprised how manyemployers don't have a current and up to date disciplinary and grievance procedure.
10. Put aside 500 euros as a slush fund if you have to engage the services of a lawyer.
11. Have a slush fund that can keep you and your family afloat for three months if you have no choice but to walk out of your job.
12. IF you have to sacrifice your values, health (including mental) and your family then you are in the wrong job. So move on.
13. Have a vision for your life.

Scripture: "So God created man in His own image; in the image of God." (Genesis 1 v 27)

Lesson: At this stage you realise your employer has sold you a big fat lie. 2021 is when that lie ends and you change course.

Exercise: Out of ten, how likely are you to FULLY embrace at least five of these guidelines in the next twelve months.

Chapter 21
A Paradigm Shift

1. Introduction

I mentioned that one of the five-fold objectives of this book was for employers to see employees as assets. What has this got to do with bullying? Bully boy authoritarian leaders in the work-place are about to become obsolete in this decade. The year is 2021, and if you don't have that perspective then you are a complete moron. You WILL go out of business eventually unless you change your attitude. If you knew that every employee could increase you profitability by two per cent, by acknowledging that they have ideas that could improve your business, would you CHANGE your attitude?

The coronavirus has given many people, including employers, a whole new perspective on life. Some of you reading this have gone out of business. If you were to start a business again, would you have a new perspective on employees in your company? I wanted this book on bullying in the workplace to *dovetail into solutions* at the end of the book. Those solutions will come from employees, employers and the legal profession.

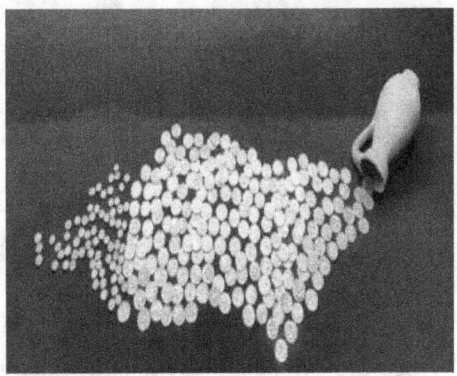

1. Six pointers to unlocking the treasure in your employees

With limited resources, employers must learn to use and leverage their employee's talent to the max. Most employers are oblivious to the fact that they are sitting on a treasure trove of untapped talent. Employers need to shift their focus from top-down and look at the organisation as a whole. [67]

---

[67] Don MaruskaandJayPerry (https://www.entrepreneur.com/article/231623)

a) <u>Power up your talent story</u>

Talent is simply not just your strengths or your skill set. It is how you express yourself. The potential of that self-expression lives in the stories you share.[68]

b) <u>Accelerate through obstacles.</u>

Find inspiration by using obstacles as talent accelerators. Talent needs obstacles to realise its full potential. [69]

c) <u>Leaders must encourage their organisations</u>

"*…to dance to forms of music, yet to be heard,*" according to Warren Bennis. Being able to have a clear overview of the organisation enables leaders to see where there are resources within the company that could be put to use. Since these human resources are already present and mostly cost-free, consider tapping into this talent pool as opposed to outsourcing. [70]

---

[68] https://blog.impraise.com/360-feedback/three-steps-you-can-take-to-unlock-your-teams-full-thepotential-360-feedback
[69] Ibid 67
[70] https://blog.impraise.com/360-feedback/three-steps-you-can-take-to-unlock-your-teams-full-thepotential-360-feedback AND https://www.octanner.com/insights/articles/2020/3/2/_5_hr_challenges_5_w.hml

d) <u>Help employees discover their purpose</u>

William Joyce, philosopher and founder of modern psychology, delivered a great speech at the American Philosophical Association at Columbia University in 1906. The Speech, which is still valid and valuable, focuses on the importance of achieving one's true potential. [71]

e) <u>Create a superstar team</u>

According Todd Carlisle, Google's former staffing manager, you should hire people who would have "fitted in when Sergey Brin and Larry Page were using a Ping-Pong table as a conference table." Carlisle looks for *"raw intellect, learning agility, diversity, leadership and innovation in resumes."* [72]

---

[71] https://www.uky.edu/~eushe2/Pajares/jamesPeace1904.html
[72] https://www.forbes.com/sites/davidsturt/2018/03/08/10-shocking-workplace-stats-you-need-to-know/#5bd00104f3af

f) <u>Recognition</u> is the number one thing employees say their manager could give them to inspire them to produce great work. Global studies prove that when it comes to inspiring people to be their best at work, nothing else comes close, "not even higher pay, promotion, autonomy or training," than encouragement.[73]

Scripture: *"Therefore encourage and build each other up."* (1 Thessalonians 5 v 11).

Lesson: Just show appreciation when somebody does a good job.

Exercise: Out of ten, how likely are you to show appreciation to your co-worker.

---

[73]https://www.octanner.com/insights/articles/2019/4/15/_9_questions_to_ask_.html

Chapter 22
The Legal Profession

1. Introduction

In order to shake up the current legal landscape in the area of litigation costs for employees, I am proposing to the legal profession in Ireland to get behind a push for legal aid up to the value of 5,000 euros for employees who simply cannot afford the legal costs. This legal aid will be for either WRC hearings or Labour Court proceedings. I will be advocating for the amendment of section 27 (2) of the 1995 Civil Legal Aid Act The prohibitive cost of legal services is a real barrier to the <u>effective access to justice</u> for the majority of individuals in society, and that means that only some groups are in a position to have access to legal counsel.

1. Let's quickly view the various bodies who can afford to go to court.

(a) Corporate entities such as private sector companies and public bodies such as local authorities and central government agencies that have resources to pay for legal services
(b) Wealthy individuals whose resources allow them to engage legal services regardless of cost.
(c) Extremely low-income individuals whose income is both very low and the subject matter of their dispute (such as family law or challenge to their immigration status) falls within the remit of the civil legal aid scheme;
(d) Individuals whose personal injuries claim is denied sufficient merit by a solicitor and counsel that it is taken on a deferred fee basis.
(e) Individuals with an unusual public interest claim that a solicitor and counsel will take on a pro bonus basis and
(f) Persons charged with criminal offences that come within the state funded criminal-aid-scheme. [74]

---

[74] Byrne and Mc Cutcheon, Irish legal Systems, Bloomsbury (6th edn 2014) p 418-419

So again, it is the middle classes who are most disadvantaged when it comes to accessing justice in the Irish Judicial System. [75]

2. Conclusion

The EU Code of Ethics for Lawyers and the International Bar Association makes it clear that lawyers should seek the most cost-effective solution for their clients. [76] And finally, wise words from the Australian legal system *"An effective Justice System must be accessible in all parts. Without this, the system risks losing its relevance to and respect of the community it serves. Accessibility is about more than the ease of access to sandstone buildings or getting legal advice. It involves an appreciation of the needs of those who require the assistance of the legal system."* [77]

I have set up an online campaign for the matter of a legal aid budget of 5,000 euro to be allocated to employees at the WRC or Labour Court stage for families who earn up to 60,000 euros.

---

[75] The Honourable Warren K. Winkler Chief Justice of Ontario, Access to Justice, Mediation: Panacea or Pariah (2007) www.ontariocourts.ca/coa) and Civil Legal Aid Act 1995

[76] Rule 3.7.1 of the CBBE Code of conduct for Lawyers in the European Union and Rule 11 of the International Bar Association International Code of Ethics

[77] Report by the Access to Justice Taskforce "A Strategic Framework for Access to Justice in the Federal Civil Justice System" (Department of the Attorney General of Australia, 2009) Available at www.ag.gov.au.

Click on the link below and let's get the ball rolling to meet the needs of those who require the assistance of the legal system.

It is on https://www.petitions.net. The name of the petition is '5,000 euro of Free Legal Aid for Employees in Litigation circumstances' [78]

Scripture: *"If anyone then knows the good they ought to do and doesn't do it, it is sin for them."* (James 4 v 17)

Lesson: Don't make the mistakes of past generations by procrastinating.

Exercise: Out of ten, what is the likelihood of lawyers in Ireland pushing for a 5,000-euro legal package for employees in an employment battle with their employer?

---

[78]https://www.petitions.net/5000_euro_of_free_legal_aid_for_employees_in_litigation_battles_with_employer?u=4827278&uv=22002638

CONCLUSION

It has been a privilege to write this book. It has been a labour of love. That said, we must ask the question of what we have learned about the central topic of bullying at work. The research is clear that this is a silent but deadly epidemic. The effect will be felt in another decade with another revolution in the workplace. You will see more people self-employed than ever. With regard to empowering employees to tackle this monster, only time will tell how impactful this book has been. For employers, I pray that the coronavirus Epidemic has shown you how amazing and brave your employees were in the midst of this monster of an epidemic.

And finally, what about the legal profession in Ireland? The Irish Law Society and the Bar Council have a marvellous opportunity to bring change, level the playing field and ensure employees have a fighting chance in a litigation situation. Let 2022 be the year that marked a profound change in Ireland where the Irish people said they had enough of bullying in the workplace. Let us use the sudden economic crash caused by the coronavirus to reflect on how we interact in the employment arena. Let us value people above material wealth from here on in!

<u>So how did you score in the overall questionnaire?</u>

80-105 – You need to take baby steps and start implementing some of the advice and counsel in this book to turn your life around. God wants you to thrive and not just survive.

105-126 – You recognise there are issues you need to deal with, don't procrastinate. Keep moving.

127-148 – This book is confirmation that you are on the right track. Well done. People are looking to you and will follow you.

149-168 – You are an influencer. Go help loads of people!

- Anthony Thuillier, *Company Law in Ireland*, Clarus Press, (2nd edn 2014)
- Byrne and Mc Cutcheon, *Irish legal Systems*, Bloomsbury (6th edn 2014)
- Christopher Dines *Drug, addiction recovery, the mindful way* (2019)
- Gerard Coffee, *Administrative Law*, Roundhall, (2nd edn 2010)
- Howard Taylor, (Schlock Mercenary, #1)*The Tub of Happiness* (The Tayler Corporation, 2007)

Ruffley v St Anne's Board of Management, (2017) IEHC 235

Cormac Doolin V The Data Protection Commissioner and Our Lady's Hospice and Care Service, {2020} IEHC 90

Deegan v Dunne's Stores {2014} 2 JIEC 2506 (Employment Appeals Tribunal)

Kielty v Minister for Social Welfare No 2 (1977) IR 267 No 2

La Moselle Clothing Ltd v Souhali {1998} 2 ILRM551

Lopez Ribalda and ORS v Spain {2019} ECHR 752

Metropolitan Properties Co (FGC) Ltd v Lannon {1968} 3 All ER 304

Orange Communications v Director of Communications (N0 2) {2000} 4 I.R 159

Quigley v Complex Tooling & Moulding {2008} IESC 44

Re Murphs Restaurant Ltd {1979} ILRM 141

Re City Equitable Fire Insurance Co {1925} Ch. 407

Zalewski v Adjudication Officer (2019) IESC 17

Law Reports

1. Report by the Access to Justice Taskforce "A Strategic Framework for Access to Justice in the Federal Civil Justice System" (Department of the Attorney General of Australia, 2009)
2. The Honourable Warren K. Winkler Chief Justice of Ontario, "Access to Justice, Mediation: Panacea or Pariah" (2007)

- Civil Legal Aid Act 1995
- Company Law Act 2014
- Data Protection Act 1988 and 2003
- Employment Equality Acts 1998-2015
- Safety, Health and Welfare at Work Act 2005 (as amended)

- Article 30.3.1
- Article 34.1
- Article 37

Dr Rob Long, Executive Director at Human Dimensions Pty Ltd, "All injuries are preventable and other silly sayings" https://safetyrisk.net/all-injuries-are-preventable-and-other-silly-safety-sayings/#comment-2582

Resources for Those Experiencing Bullying

- Your first port of call should be a G.P
- Citizens Advice bureau (https://www.citizensinformation.ie/en/contact_us.html

- Samaritans if you are feeling suicidal https://www.samaritans.org/ireland/samaritans-ireland/
- It is worth approaching a god employment lawyer – average cost would be 50/60 euro for a consultation
- My law page @cathalslawpage on Facebook

This book represents the views and opinions of the author. For professional legal advice please speak to a qualified lawyer. Every effort has been made to ensure that the content of this book is factual and up to date and that it is not defamatory in any way. I have made every effort to ensure it respects and abides by the legislation laid down in the Defamation Act of 2009 in Ireland.

www.ingramcontent.com/pod-product-compliance
Lightning Source LLC
Chambersburg PA
CBHW060414220526
45465CB00008B/2878